New Roads and Street Works Act 1991

CHAPTER 22

Explanatory Notes are available separately

GRAN*GIS* UK Publishing

Adapted and published by GRANGIS (Grand Register Library).
Online: www.grangis.com
E-mail: contact@grangis.com

In this version:
ISBN: 979-8-88559-029-7

Note: This is the original version (as it was originally enacted). Title, sub-title and the generated date is as marked on the pages.

New Roads and Street Works Act 1991

CHAPTER 22

NEW ROADS AND STREET WORKS ACT 1991

PART I

NEW ROADS IN ENGLAND AND WALES

Concession agreements

Toll orders

Further provisions with respect to tolls

Notice and co-ordination of works

Roads subject to special controls

General requirements as to execution of road works

Reinstatement

Charges, fees and contributions payable by undertakers

Duties and liabilities of undertakers with respect to apparatus

Apparatus affected by road, bridge or transport works

Provisions with respect to particular authorities and undertakings

Pipelines Act 1962 (c. 58)

101 (1) The Pipelines Act 1962 is amended as follows.

New Towns (Scotland) Act 1968 (c. 16)

102 In section 8 of the New Towns (Scotland) Act 1968...

Sewerage (Scotland) Act 1968 (c. 47)

103 (1) The Sewerage (Scotland) Act 1968 is amended as follows....

Town and Country Planning (Scotland) Act 1972 (c. 52)

104 In section 209(2) of the Town and Country Planning (Scotland)...

Control of Pollution Act 1974 (c. 40)

105 In section 105(1) of the Control of Pollution Act 1974...

Local Government (Miscellaneous Provisions) Act 1976 (c. 57)

106 In section 15 of the Local Government (Miscellaneous Provisions) Act...

Development of Rural Wales Act 1976 (c. 75)

107 In Schedule 3 to the Development of Rural Wales Act...

Water (Scotland) Act 1980 (c. 45)

108 (1) The Water (Scotland) Act 1980 is amended as follows....

Local Government, Planning and Land Act 1980 (c. 65)

109 In section 167 of the Local Government, Planning and Land...

Water Act 1981 (c. 12)

110 In section 6 of the Water Act 1981 (liability of...

British Telecommunications Act 1981 (c. 38)

111 In Schedule 3 to the British Telecommunications Act 1981, in...

New Towns Act 1981 (c. 64)

112 In section 11 of the New Towns Act 1981 (acquisition...

Telecommunications Act 1984 (c. 12)

113 (1) In Schedule 2 to the Telecommunications Act 1984 (the...
114 In the same Schedule, in paragraph 2(8)(a) (construction of references...
115 (1) In the same Schedule, paragraph 9 (street works) is...

Local Government Act 1985 (c. 51)

116 (1) In Schedule 5 to the Local Government Act 1985,...

New Roads and Street Works Act 1991

1991 CHAPTER 22

An Act to amend the law relating to roads so as to enable new roads to be provided by new means; to make new provision with respect to street works and, in Scotland, road works; and for connected purposes. [27th June 1991]

Be it enacted by the Queen's most Excellent Majesty, by and with the advice and consent of the Lords Spiritual and Temporal, and Commons, in this present Parliament assembled, and by the authority of the same, as follows:—

PART I

NEW ROADS IN ENGLAND AND WALES

Concession agreements

1 Concession agreements

(1) In this Part a "concession agreement" means an agreement entered into by a highway authority under which a person (the "concessionaire"), in return for undertaking such obligations as may be specified in the agreement with respect to the design, construction, maintenance, operation or improvement of a special road, is appointed to enjoy the right (conferred or to be conferred by a toll order under this Part) to charge tolls in respect of the use of the road.

References in this Part to a concession agreement are to the agreement as varied or supplemented from time to time.

(2) Except as otherwise expressly provided by this Part, the provisions of the Highways Act 1980 apply in relation to a special road in relation to which a concession agreement is in force (referred to in this Part as a "road subject to a concession") as in relation to any other special road provided or to be provided by the highway authority.

(3) A concession agreement shall provide that any land held by the concessionaire which in the opinion of the highway authority is required, in connection with the matters provided for in the agreement, for any purpose for which the authority may acquire land under Part XII of the Highways Act 1980 shall be transferred to the highway authority without payment.

(4) A concession agreement relating to the design and construction of a special road shall provide that if the special road scheme authorising the provision of the road is not made or confirmed, or if the highway authority decide not to proceed with the proposed road, the authority shall pay to the concessionaire such compensation in respect of costs incurred by him as may be determined in accordance with the agreement.

(5) A concession agreement relating to the design and construction of a special road shall provide that if the concessionaire fails to complete the road in accordance with the agreement, he shall, without prejudice to any other liability, pay to the highway authority such compensation as may be determined in accordance with the agreement in respect of costs incurred by them.

Those costs shall be taken to include the relevant administrative expenses of the authority, including an appropriate sum in respect of general staff costs and overheads.

2 Exercise of highway functions by concessionaire

(1) A concession agreement may authorise the concessionaire to exercise in place of the highway authority such highway functions to which this section applies as may be specified in the agreement.

(2) For this purpose "highway functions" means all functions in relation to the road subject to the concession which are exercisable, in whatever capacity, by the authority who are the highway authority; and this section applies to all such functions, except—

(a) powers to make schemes or orders under the Highways Act 1980,

(b) powers to make regulations or orders, or give directions, under the Road Traffic Regulation Act 1984, and

(c) such other functions as may be prescribed by the Secretary of State by regulations.

(3) A highway function exercisable by the concessionaire may be exercised by the highway authority themselves only—

(a) in an emergency, or

(b) if it appears to the authority that such exercise is necessary or expedient in the interests of road safety, or

(c) if it appears to the authority that the concessionaire has failed or is unable properly to discharge the function in any respect;

and the highway authority shall not be liable for anything done or omitted by the concessionaire in the exercise or purported exercise of a highway function.

(4) The highway authority may recover from the concessionaire the costs incurred by them in exercising in the circumstances mentioned in subsection (3)(a), (b) or (c) a highway function exercisable by the concessionaire.

Those costs shall be taken to include the relevant administrative expenses of the authority, including an appropriate sum in respect of general staff costs and overheads.

(5) The concessionaire shall in the exercise of a highway function act in accordance with the terms of the concession agreement; and the agreement may provide for the withdrawal of the concessionaire's authority to exercise any such function.

(6) Regulations under this section shall be made by statutory instrument which shall be subject to annulment in pursuance of a resolution of either House of Parliament.

3 Provisions as to traffic regulation

(1) The following provisions have effect with respect to the operation of the Road Traffic Regulation Act 1984 ("the 1984 Act") in relation to a road subject to a concession.

(2) The traffic authority shall consult the concessionaire before making any regulations or order under the 1984 Act specifically relating to the road.

(3) The concessionaire may cause or permit traffic signs (within the meaning of section 64(1) of the 1984 Act) to be placed on or near the road, but subject to any directions given by the traffic authority.

If the concessionaire fails to comply with a direction of the traffic authority as to the placing of traffic signs, the authority may themselves carry out the work required and recover from the concessionaire the expenses reasonably incurred by them in doing so.

(4) The concessionaire may issue a notice under section 14 of the 1984 Act (temporary restriction or prohibition of traffic) having the same effect as a notice issued under that section by the traffic authority.

The Secretary of State may by regulations make provision excluding in relation to such a notice issued by a concessionaire the provisions of the 1984 Act relating to—

(a) the procedure in connection with the issue of the notice,

(b) the maximum duration of the notice, and

(c) the making of provision in relation to alternative roads,

and making instead such other provision as appears to him to be appropriate.

(5) A notice issued by the concessionaire by virtue of subsection (4) may be revoked or varied by the traffic authority and shall cease to have effect if provision inconsistent with it is made by that authority by order or notice under section 14 of the 1984 Act.

(6) Regulations under this section shall be made by statutory instrument which shall be subject to annulment in pursuance of a resolution of either House of Parliament.

4 Leasing of land to concessionaire

(1) A highway authority who have entered into a concession agreement may grant to the concessionaire a lease of any land if it appears to the authority to be expedient to do so for the purpose of or in connection with the exercise by the concessionaire of his functions under the agreement.

(2) No enactment or rule of law regulating the rights and obligations of landlords and tenants shall prejudice the operation of an agreement between the authority and the concessionaire as to the terms on which land which is the subject of a lease granted under subsection (1) is provided for the concessionaire's use.

(3) Accordingly no such enactment or rule of law applies in relation to the rights and obligations of the parties to a lease so granted—

(a) so as to exclude or modify in any respect any of the rights and obligations of those parties under the terms of the lease, whether with respect to the termination of the tenancy or any other matter;

(b) so as to confer or impose on either party any right or obligation arising out of or connected with anything done or omitted on or in relation to land which is the subject of the lease, in addition to any such right or obligation provided for by the terms of the lease;

(c) so as to restrict the enforcement (whether by action for damages or otherwise) by either party to the lease of any obligation of the other party under the lease.

5 Transfer or termination of concession

(1) The rights of a concessionaire under a concession agreement may be assigned with the consent of the highway authority; and references in this Part to the concessionaire shall be construed as references to the person for the time being entitled to exercise those rights.

(2) On the termination of a concession agreement (by effluxion of time or otherwise) there shall be transferred to the highway authority by virtue of this section all such property, rights and liabilities of the concessionaire as in accordance with the concession agreement fall to be so transferred in the circumstances.

Schedule 1 contains supplementary provisions with respect to that transfer.

(3) Where a concession agreement terminates or is terminated before the end of the toll period, the highway authority—

(a) shall take reasonable steps to secure the appointment of a new concessionaire, and

(b) may, for a period of not more than two years until a new appointment or an extension toll order takes effect or the toll period ends, charge and collect tolls in the same way as a concessionaire.

(4) A concession agreement may contain provision as to the circumstances in which, and extent to which, any sum received by the highway authority—

(a) in consideration for the appointment of a new concessionaire, or

(b) by way of tolls collected by virtue of subsection (3)(b),

is to be applied for the benefit of the former concessionaire or his creditors, as the case may be.

Toll orders

6 Toll orders

(1) An order authorising the charging of tolls (a "toll order") may be made in relation to a special road proposed to be provided by a highway authority.

The order shall state whether it authorises the charging of tolls by a concessionaire or by the highway authority.

(2) A toll order relating to a special road to be provided by the Secretary of State shall be made by the Secretary of State; and a toll order relating to a special road to be provided by a local highway authority shall be made by the authority and confirmed by the Secretary of State.

(3) Schedule 2 has effect as to the making or confirmation of a toll order and as to its validity and date of operation.

(4) The proceedings required to be taken in relation to a toll order shall (so far as practicable) be taken concurrently with the proceedings required to be taken under the Highways Act 1980 in relation to the special road scheme authorising the provision of the road to which the order relates.

(5) The Secretary of State shall not make or confirm the scheme or the toll order unless he makes or confirms them both.

(6) The power conferred on the Secretary of State by this section to make or confirm a toll order is exercisable by statutory instrument.

7 The toll period

(1) A toll order shall provide for tolls to be chargeable for a period (the "toll period") specified in or determined in accordance with the order.

(2) The order may provide for the toll period to end—

(a) on a date, or at the end of a period, specified in the order, or

(b) on a date determined by reference to—

(i) the achievement of a specified financial objective, or

(ii) the passage of a specified number of vehicles,

or such other factors, or combinations of factors, as may be specified in the order, or

(c) on whichever is the earlier or later of dates specified in or determined in accordance with the order.

(3) In the case of a toll order authorising the charging of tolls by a concessionaire, it is for the highway authority to decide any matter relevant to determining the date on which the toll period ends.

8 Amount of tolls chargeable by concessionaire

(1) A toll order authorising the charging of tolls by a concessionaire shall specify the maximum tolls which may be charged if, and only if, the road to which the order relates consists of or includes a major crossing to which there is no reasonably convenient alternative.

(2) The Secretary of State may make provision by regulations as to what is to be treated as a major crossing for this purpose and as to the circumstances in which another route is to be taken to be, or not to be, a reasonably convenient alternative.

(3) Subject to any such regulations, a major crossing means a crossing of navigable waters more than 100 metres wide and a reasonably convenient alternative means another crossing (other than a ferry) which is free of toll and is within five miles of the crossing in question.

For this purpose—

(a) the width of tidal waters shall be ascertained by reference to the mean high-water mark and the width of other waters by reference to the ordinary limits of the waters, and

(b) the distance between two crossings shall be taken to be the shortest distance between the centre lines of the two crossings.

(4) The order shall specify the maximum tolls which may be charged for the use of the crossing or any length of the road including the crossing; and if the condition as to absence of a reasonably convenient alternative is satisfied in relation to certain types of traffic only, the order shall make provision only in relation to those types of traffic.

If that condition ceases to be satisfied, generally or in relation to certain types of traffic, the provisions of the order as to maximum tolls shall cease to apply, or cease to apply to that type of traffic, for so long as that remains the case.

(5) The order may specify different maxima for different descriptions of traffic (which need not correspond with the classes of traffic prescribed by the special road scheme) and may provide for the amounts to be varied in accordance with a formula specified in the order.

(6) Regulations under this section shall be made by statutory instrument and shall not be made unless a draft of them has been laid before and approved by a resolution of each House of Parliament.

Any regulations so made do not apply in relation to an order if notice of the draft order, and of the relevant draft special road scheme, have been published before the regulations come into force.

9 Amount of tolls chargeable by highway authority

(1) A toll order authorising the charging of tolls by the highway authority shall in every case specify the maximum tolls which may be charged for the use of the road or any length of the road in respect of which tolls are charged.

(2) The order may specify different maxima for different descriptions of traffic (which need not correspond with the classes of traffic prescribed by the special road scheme) and may provide for the amounts to be varied in accordance with a formula specified in the order.

10 Application of enactments relating to monopolies, &c

(1) For the purposes of—

(a) the Fair Trading Act 1973,

(b) the provisions of the Competition Act 1980 relating to anti-competitive practices, and

(c) the provisions of the Restrictive Trade Practices Act 1976 relating to restrictive agreements,

a person authorised by a toll order to charge tolls shall be deemed to supply a service, namely, providing the facility to use the road in return for the toll charged.

(2) Where the toll charged is subject to a maximum specified by the toll order, the Fair Trading Act 1973 has effect—

(a) as if the service deemed by subsection (1) above to be supplied were among those listed in Part I of Schedule 7 to that Act (services excluded from Director's power to make monopoly reference), and

(b) as if, in relation to any such service, the Secretary of State for Transport were among the Ministers listed in section 51(3) of that Act (Ministers whose concurrence is required for monopoly reference by the Secretary of State).

(3) The Restrictive Trade Practices Act 1976 has effect in relation to any agreement which—

(a) was made before the date on which this section comes into force, and

(b) becomes subject to registration under that Act on that date by virtue of the effect which an order under section 11 of that Act has as a result of the coming into force of this section,

as if the agreement had become subject to registration by virtue of an order under that section coming into force on that date.

In this subsection "agreement" has the same meaning as in that Act.

11 Variation or revocation of toll order

(1) A toll order may be varied or revoked—

(a) by an order made by the Secretary of State if he is the highway authority for the road, and

(b) by an order made by the highway authority and confirmed by the Secretary of State in any other case.

(2) The Secretary of State may confirm an order made by another authority either without modifications or subject to such modifications as he thinks fit.

(3) A toll order may not be varied so as to extend the toll period; and a toll order which does not authorise the charging of tolls in respect of the whole length of the special road to which it relates may not be varied so as to extend the length of road in respect of which tolls may be charged.

(4) A toll order relating to a road subject to a concession may not be varied or revoked without the consent of the concessionaire.

(5) An order under this section may contain such supplementary, incidental and transitional provisions as appear to the highway authority to be necessary or expedient.

(6) An order under this section made by the Secretary of State, and an instrument made by the Secretary of State confirming an order under this section made by another authority, shall be made by statutory instrument which shall be subject to annulment in pursuance of a resolution of either House of Parliament.

The provisions of Schedule 2 (procedure in connection with toll orders) do not apply.

12 Extension toll orders

(1) An order authorising the charging of tolls by the highway authority (an "extension toll order") may be made in relation to a road which is or has been subject to a concession.

(2) An extension toll order relating to a special road for which the Secretary of State is the highway authority shall be made by the Secretary of State; and an extension toll

order relating to a road for which the highway authority is a local highway authority shall be made by that authority and confirmed by the Secretary of State.

(3) Any extension toll order must be made so as to come into force not later than—

(a) the end of the toll period under the previous toll order, or

(b) where the concession agreement terminates or is terminated before the end of that period, two years after the termination of the agreement,

whichever is the earlier.

(4) The following provisions of this Act apply in relation to an extension toll order as in relation to a toll order under section 6(1)—

section 7(1) and (2) (the toll period),
section 9 (amount of tolls chargeable by highway authority),
section 10 (application of enactments relating to monopolies, &c.),
section 11 (variation or revocation of order),
sections 13 to 17 (further provisions with respect to tolls), and
section 18 (annual report by Secretary of State).

(5) An extension toll order made by the Secretary of State, and an instrument made by the Secretary of State confirming an extension toll order made by a local highway authority, shall be made by statutory instrument which shall be subject to annulment in pursuance of a resolution of either House of Parliament.

The provisions of Schedule 2 (procedure in connection with toll orders) do not apply.

Further provisions with respect to tolls

13 Further provisions as to charging of tolls

(1) A toll order may contain provision exempting from liability for tolls such descriptions of traffic as may be specified in the order.

This does not affect the power of the person authorised by the order to charge tolls to grant such other exemptions from toll as he thinks fit.

(2) A toll order shall contain provision exempting from liability to pay any toll—

(a) a police vehicle, identifiable as such by writing or markings on it or otherwise by its appearance, if being used for police purposes;

(b) an ambulance as defined in section 4(2) of the Vehicles (Excise) Act 1971;

(c) a fire engine as so defined;

(d) a vehicle exempt from duty under that Act by virtue of—

section 4(1)(g) of that Act (invalid carriages),

section 4(1)(kb) of that Act (vehicles used for carriage of disabled persons by recognised bodies), or

section 7(2) of that Act (vehicles used by or for purposes of disabled person).

(3) A person authorised by a toll order to charge tolls may, subject to the provisions of the order—

(a) suspend the collection of tolls;

(b) enter into agreements under which persons compound in advance, on such terms as may be agreed, for the payment of tolls;
(c) charge different tolls according to—
(i) the distance travelled, or
(ii) the day, time of day, week, month or other period; and
(d) charge different tolls for different descriptions of traffic.

In the case of a concessionaire the powers mentioned above are exercisable subject to the provisions of the concession agreement.

14 Collection of tolls

(1) The Secretary of State may make provision by regulations with respect to the collection of tolls in pursuance of a toll order.

(2) Different provision may be made for different types of road or different types of toll, or for particular roads or particular tolls.

(3) Regulations may, in particular, impose requirements with respect to—
(a) the displaying of lists of tolls, and
(b) the manner of implementing changes in the amount of tolls;

and where any such requirements are imposed, a toll may not be demanded unless they are, or as the case may be have been, complied with.

(4) A person who in respect of the use of a road to which a toll order relates demands a toll—
(a) which he is not authorised to charge, or
(b) which by virtue of subsection (3) may not be demanded,

commits an offence and is liable on summary conviction to a fine not exceeding level 3 on the standard scale.

(5) Regulations under this section shall be made by statutory instrument which shall be subject to annulment in pursuance of a resolution of either House of Parliament.

15 Refusal or failure to pay tolls

(1) A person who without reasonable excuse refuses or fails to pay, or who attempts to evade payment of, a toll which he is liable to pay by virtue of a toll order commits an offence and is liable on summary conviction to a fine not exceeding level 3 on the standard scale.

(2) If it appears to a person employed for the purpose of collecting tolls that a person has, without reasonable excuse, refused or failed to pay a toll which he is liable to pay by virtue of a toll order, he may—
(a) refuse to permit him to pass, or prevent him from passing, through any place at which tolls are payable, and
(b) require him to remove his vehicle from any such place by a particular route, and if he does not comply with such a requirement cause the vehicle to be so removed;

and for the purpose of exercising the powers conferred by this subsection, a person employed for the purpose of the collection of tolls may call upon such assistance as he thinks necessary.

(3) Where a person does not comply with a requirement under subsection (2)(b) as to the removal of his vehicle, he is liable to pay a prescribed charge in respect of the removal of the vehicle.

(4) Where there remains unpaid—

(a) a toll which a person is liable to pay by virtue of a toll order, or

(b) a prescribed charge which he is liable to pay by virtue of subsection (3),

the person authorised to charge tolls may recover from the person liable the amount of the toll or charge together with a reasonable sum to cover administrative expenses.

(5) In this section a "prescribed charge" means such charge as may be specified in, or calculated in accordance with, regulations made by the Secretary of State.

The regulations may provide for the amount of the charge, or any amount used for the purpose of calculating the charge, to be varied in accordance with a formula specified in the regulations.

(6) Regulations under this section shall be made by statutory instrument which shall be subject to annulment in pursuance of a resolution of either House of Parliament.

16 Facilities for collection of tolls

(1) A person authorised by a toll order to charge tolls may set up and maintain facilities for the collection of tolls.

The consent of the highway authority is required for the setting up of any such facilities by a concessionaire.

(2) Those responsible for the design and construction of facilities for the collection of tolls, and those responsible for the collection of tolls at such facilities, shall have due regard to the need to avoid delaying the passage of such vehicles as are mentioned in section 13(2)(a), (b) or (c) (police vehicles, ambulances and fire engines).

(3) The power of the highway authority under section 239(4)(c) of the Highways Act 1980 to acquire land for the provision of buildings or facilities to be used in connection with the use of the special road includes, in the case of a road subject to a toll order, power to acquire any land required for the purpose of setting up facilities for the collection of tolls.

(4) Facilities for the collection of tolls are exempt from rating and shall not be included in any rating list.

(5) In this section "facilities for the collection of tolls" means such buildings, structures or other facilities within the boundary of the road, or on land adjoining the road, as are reasonably required for the purpose of or in connection with the collection of tolls in pursuance of a toll order.

17 Restriction of access to toll roads

(1) Where a toll order is in force in relation to a road, no highway or private means of access to premises shall be so constructed as to afford access to the road except with the consent of the highway authority and, where the road is subject to a concession, of the concessionaire.

(2) Subsection (1) does not apply to the construction of a highway or private means of access by or on behalf of a government department or Minister of the Crown which the department or Minister is satisfied is reasonably required for discharging any function of the department or Minister.

Annual Report

18 Annual report on concession agreements and toll orders

(1) The Secretary of State shall in respect of each calendar year lay before Parliament a report—

(a) stating the number of concession agreements entered into by him during that year,

(b) stating the number of new roads opened to public use during that year for which he is the highway authority and which at the time of their opening were subject to a concession,

(c) listing the toll orders, and orders varying or revoking toll orders, made or confirmed by him in that year, and

(d) containing such information as appears to him to be appropriate with respect to the toll orders (whenever made) which are in force during that year or any part of it.

(2) The report shall be laid on or before 31st July in the following calendar year.

Miscellaneous

19 Environmental assessment of projects involving special roads

In section 105A of the Highways Act 1980 (environmental assessment of certain highway projects), after subsection (2) (cases in which environmental statement must be published) insert—

"(2A) Any project for the construction or improvement of a special road which falls within Annex II to the Directive shall be treated as having such characteristics that it should be made subject to an environmental assessment in accordance with the Directive.".

20 Classification of traffic for purposes of special roads

(1) In section 17 of the Highways Act 1980 (classification of traffic for purposes of special roads), in subsection (3) omit the words from "and references" to the end (which relate to the effect of an amending order on existing schemes) and after that subsection insert—

"(4) An amending order may contain provision applying the amendments made by the order to existing schemes (whether made by the Minister or a local highway authority); and in the absence of such provision an amending order does not affect the classes of traffic prescribed in an existing scheme.

In this subsection an "existing scheme" means a scheme under section 16 made before the order comes into operation.".

(2) In section 325 of the Highways Act 1980 (provisions as to orders, &c.)—

(a) omit subsection (3) (which requires affirmative resolution for an order under section 17 varying the classes of traffic for the purposes of special roads); and

(b) in subsection (2)(b) (orders subject to negative resolution), after "section" insert "17 above or".

21 Certain special roads not necessarily trunk roads

(1) In section 19 of the Highways Act 1980 (under which a special road provided by the Secretary of State becomes a trunk road), after subsection (2) add—

"(3) Subsections (1) and (2) above have effect subject to any provision of the scheme under section 16 directing that the special road in question or any part of it shall not be a trunk road.

Any such provision does not affect the power of the Minister to make an order under section 10(2)(a) with respect to the special road or part.".

(2) In section 1(1) of the Highways Act 1980 (highways for which the Minister is the highway authority), after paragraph (a) (trunk roads) insert—

"(aa) any special road provided by him;".

(3) In section 2 of the Highways Act 1980 (responsibility of local highway authority for roads ceasing to be trunk roads), make the present provision subsection (1) and after it insert—

"(2) In the case of a special road provided by the Minister, subsection (1) above has effect subject to any provision of the order directing that the Minister shall continue to be the highway authority for the road.".

22 Adoption of privately constructed roads

(1) In section 38 of the Highways Act 1980 (power of highway authorities to adopt by agreement), for subsection (3) (adoption by local highway authority of private road or way) substitute—

"(3) A local highway authority may agree with any person to undertake the maintenance of a way—

(a) which that person is willing and has the necessary power to dedicate as a highway, or

(b) which is to be constructed by that person, or by a highway authority on his behalf, and which he proposes to dedicate as a highway;

and where an agreement is made under this subsection the way to which the agreement relates shall, on such date as may be specified in the agreement, become for the purposes of this Act a highway maintainable at the public expense.

(3A) The Minister may agree with any person to undertake the maintenance of a road—

(a) which that person is willing and has the necessary power to dedicate as a highway, or

(b) which is to be constructed by that person, or by a highway authority on his behalf, and which he proposes to dedicate as a highway,

and which the Minister proposes should become a trunk road; and where an agreement is made under this subsection the road shall become for the purposes of this Act a highway maintainable at the public expense on the date on which an order comes into force under section 10 directing that the road become a trunk road or, if later, the date on which the road is opened for the purposes of through traffic.".

(2) In section 10 of the Highways Act 1980 (general provisions as to trunk roads)—

(a) in subsection (2)(a) (highways which may be made trunk roads) for ", or any highway proposed to be constructed by the Minister," substitute—

"or any proposed highway—

(i) to be constructed by the Minister, or

(ii) in relation to which the Minister has entered or proposes to enter into an agreement under section 38(3A),";

(b) in subsection (4) omit the words from "Without prejudice" to the end of paragraph (b), for "highway proposed to be constructed by the Minister" substitute "proposed highway" and omit "by the Minister" in the second place where it occurs; and

(c) in subsection (7) for "highway proposed to be constructed by the Minister" substitute "proposed highway".

23 Execution of works by highway authority at expense of another

In Part XIII of the Highways Act 1980 (financial provisions), for section 278 (contributions by persons deriving special benefit from works) substitute—

"278 Agreements as to execution of works

(1) A highway authority may, if they are satisfied it will be of benefit to the public, enter into an agreement with any person—

(a) for the execution by the authority of any works which the authority are or may be authorised to execute, or

(b) for the execution by the authority of such works incorporating particular modifications, additions or features, or at a particular time or in a particular manner,

on terms that that person pays the whole or such part of the cost of the works as may be specified in or determined in accordance with the agreement.

(2) Without prejudice to the generality of the reference in subsection (1) to the cost of the works, that reference shall be taken to include—

(a) the whole of the costs incurred by the highway authority in or in connection with—

(i) the making of the agreement,

(ii) the making or confirmation of any scheme or order required for the purposes of the works,

(iii) the granting of any authorisation, permission or consent required for the purposes of the works, and

(iv) the acquisition by the authority of any land required for the purposes of the works; and

(b) all relevant administrative expenses of the highway authority, including an appropriate sum in respect of general staff costs and overheads.

(3) The agreement may also provide for the making to the highway authority of payments in respect of the maintenance of the works to which the agreement relates and may contain such incidental and consequential provisions as appear to the highway authority to be necessary or expedient for the purposes of the agreement.

(4) The fact that works are to be executed in pursuance of an agreement under this section does not affect the power of the authority to acquire land, by agreement or compulsorily, for the purposes of the works.

(5) If any amount due to a highway authority in pursuance of an agreement under this section is not paid in accordance with the agreement, the authority may—

(a) direct that any means of access or other facility afforded by the works to which the agreement relates shall not be used until that amount has been paid,

(b) recover that amount from any person having an estate or interest in any land for the benefit of which any such means of access or other facility is afforded, and

(c) declare that amount to be a charge on any such land (identifying it) and on all estates and interests therein.

(6) If it appears to the highway authority that a direction under subsection (5)(a) is not being complied with, the authority may execute such works as are necessary to stop up the means of access or deny the facility, as the case may be, and may for that purpose enter any land.

(7) Where a highway authority recovers an amount from a person by virtue of subsection (5)(b), he may in turn recover from any other person having an estate or interest in land for the benefit of which the means of access or other facility was afforded such contribution as may be found by the court to be just and equitable.

This does not affect the right of any of those persons to recover from the person liable under the agreement the amount which they are made to pay.

(8) The Local Land Charges Act 1975 applies in relation to a charge under subsection (5)(c) in favour of the Secretary of State as in relation to a charge in favour of a local authority.".

24 Exercise of road traffic regulation powers

In Part X of the Road Traffic Regulation Act 1984 (general and supplementary provisions), after section 122 insert—

"122A Prospective exercise of powers

(1) Any power under this Act to make an order or give a direction may be exercised before the road to which it relates is open for public use, so as to take effect immediately on the road's becoming open for public use.

(2) The procedure for making an order or giving a direction applies in such a case with such modifications as may be prescribed.".

General

25 Application of provisions of the Highways Act 1980, &c

(1) The following provisions of the Highways Act 1980 apply for the purposes of this Part as if it were a part of that Act—

section 302 (inquiries),

section 303 (penalty for obstructing execution of Act),

section 312 (restriction on institution of proceedings for offence),

section 319 (judges and justices not to be disqualified by liability to rates),

sections 320 to 322 (provisions as to notices), and

section 323 (reckoning of periods).

(2) Nothing in this Part shall be construed as restricting the powers of a highway authority with respect to a road subject to a concession—

(a) as to the matters which may be provided for in the concession agreement or as to the making of agreements of any other description for any purpose connected with the special road; or

(b) as to the acquisition, by agreement or compulsorily, of any land which in the opinion of the authority is required, in connection with the road, for any purpose for which the authority may acquire land under Part XII of the Highways Act 1980.

(3) Nothing in a concession agreement shall be construed as affecting the status of the road subject to the concession as a highway maintainable at the public expense.

26 Interpretation

(1) In this Part the following expressions have the same meaning as in the Highways Act 1980—

"highway authority",

"local highway authority",

"special road",

"special road authority", and

"traffic";

and "special road scheme" means a scheme under section 16 of that Act authorising the provision of a special road.

(2) Where a concession agreement is entered into jointly by two or more local highway authorities, references in this Part to the highway authority shall be construed—

(a) as references to each of those authorities in relation to times, circumstances and purposes before the special road scheme becomes operative, and

(b) in relation to times, circumstances and purposes after the special road scheme becomes operative, as references to the authority which in accordance with the scheme is the special road authority.

(3) The expressions listed below are defined or otherwise fall to be construed for the purposes of this Part in accordance with the provisions indicated—

concession agreement	section 1(1)
concessionaire	sections 1(1) and 5(1)
extension toll order	section 12(1)
highway authority	section 26(1) and (2)
local highway authority	section 26(1)
road subject to a concession	section 1(2)
special road	section 26(1)
special road authority	section 26(1)
special road scheme	section 26(1)
toll order	section 6
toll period	section 7
traffic	section 26(1).

PART II

NEW ROADS IN SCOTLAND

Toll Roads

27 Toll orders

(1) An order authorising the charging of tolls (a "toll order") by a roads authority may be made in relation to a special road proposed to be provided by that roads authority.

(2) A toll order relating to a special road to be provided by the Secretary of State shall be made by the Secretary of State; and a toll order relating to a special road to be provided by a local roads authority shall be made by the authority and confirmed by the Secretary of State.

(3) Part IIA, paragraphs 15 and 18 of Part III, and Part IV of Schedule 1 to the Roads (Scotland) Act 1984 apply to the making or confirmation of a toll order and Schedule 2 to that Act applies to a toll order with regard to its validity and date of operation.

(4) The proceedings required by Part IIA of Schedule 1 to that Act to be taken for the purposes of a toll order shall (so far as practicable) be taken concurrently with the proceedings required to be taken for the purposes of the special road scheme authorising the provision of the road to which the order relates.

(5) The Secretary of State shall not make or confirm the scheme or the toll order unless he makes or confirms them both.

(6) If under paragraph 3(b) of Schedule 2 to that Act the court quashes a toll order, the special road scheme for the road in respect of which the toll order was made shall also cease to have effect.

(7) Where a roads authority enter into a contract with a person for the design or construction of a road which both parties intend will be subject to a toll order, the contract shall make provision for the compensation of that person for such expenses as may be agreed in accordance with the contract in the event of—

(a) the roads authority deciding not to proceed with the special road scheme, or

(b) the Secretary of State failing to make or confirm either the toll order or the scheme.

(8) Where a roads authority enter into a contract such as is mentioned in subsection (7) above and the person who has contracted to design or construct the road fails to complete the road in accordance with the contract he shall, without prejudice to any other liability, pay the authority such compensation in respect of costs incurred by them as may be determined in accordance with the contract.

Those costs shall be taken to include the relevant administrative expenses of the authority, including an appropriate sum in respect of general staff costs and overheads.

(9) Where a toll order has been made—

(a) the road in respect of which it has been made, and

(b) such buildings, structures or other facilities within the boundary of the road or on land adjoining the road as are reasonably required for the purpose of or in connection with the collection of tolls,

are exempt from rating and shall not be included in any valuation roll.

(10) The power conferred on the Secretary of State by this section to make or confirm a toll order is exercisable by statutory instrument.

28 Assignation of rights under a toll order

(1) A toll order may authorise the special road authority in whose name it is made to assign, subject to subsection (2), to a person, for such period and subject to such terms and conditions as they think fit, their rights under a toll order to charge and to collect tolls.

(2) A special road authority may grant such an assignation only to a person who has undertaken such obligations as may be specified in the assignation with respect to the design, construction, maintenance, operation or improvement of the road.

(3) In this Part, a person to whom the rights under a toll order to charge and to collect tolls have been assigned is referred to as a concessionaire.

(4) References in this Part to a person authorised to charge tolls include references to a concessionaire.

(5) Where a special road authority grants an assignation under this section, they shall also assign to the concessionaire such income as they receive in respect of—

(a) charging for the occupation of the road,

(b) charging for any services in relation to the road other than services which they themselves have supplied, or

(c) any contribution made by a third party towards the cost of maintenance or improvement of the road,

except to the extent that they themselves have incurred expense in such cases.

(6) A special road authority shall not make a charge as mentioned in subsection (5) without consulting the concessionaire with regard to the amount to be charged in such cases as the authority has discretion as to the amount to be charged.

29 The toll period

(1) A toll order shall provide for tolls to be chargeable for a period (the "toll period") specified in or determined in accordance with the order.

(2) The order may provide for the toll period to end—

(a) on a date, or at the end of a period, specified in the order, or

(b) on a date determined by reference to—

(i) the achievement of a specified financial objective, or

(ii) the passage of a specified number of vehicles,

or such other factors, or combinations of factors, as may be specified in the order, or

(c) on whichever is the earlier or later of dates specified in or determined in accordance with the order.

(3) Where an assignation has been granted under section 28(1), it is for the special road authority to decide any matter relevant to determining the date on which the toll period ends.

30 Extension toll orders

(1) Where a toll order authorises the special road authority to assign their rights under the order to charge and collect tolls and—

(a) the authority fail to do so;

(b) such an assignation terminates or is terminated within the toll period; or

(c) the authority wish to charge and collect tolls beyond the toll period,

a further order (an "extension toll order") may be made to authorise the authority to charge and collect tolls for a new toll period.

(2) An extension toll order shall not authorise the special road authority to assign their rights under it to charge and collect tolls.

(3) An extension toll order relating to a special road for which the Secretary of State is roads authority shall be made by the Secretary of State; and an extension toll order relating to a road for which the roads authority is a local authority shall be made by that authority and confirmed by the Secretary of State.

(4) Any extension toll order must be made so as to come into force not later than—

(a) the end of the toll period under the previous toll order; or

(b) where the assignation under section 28(1) terminates or is terminated before the end of that period, two years after the termination of the assignation,

whichever is the earlier.

(5) The following provisions of this Act apply in relation to an extension toll order as in relation to a toll order under section 27(1)—

section 29(1) and (2) (the toll period)

section 31 (amount of tolls chargeable by special road authority),

section 33 (application of enactments relating to monopolies, etc.),

section 34 (variation and revocation of order),

sections 36 to 40 (further provisions with respect to tolls), and

section 41 (report by Secretary of State).

(6) The power of the Secretary of State to make or confirm an extension toll order shall be exercisable by statutory instrument which shall be subject to annulment in pursuance of a resolution of either House of Parliament; and the provisions of Schedules 1 and 2 to the Roads (Scotland) Act 1984 (procedure in connection with orders) shall not apply to an order under this section.

31 Amount of tolls chargeable

(1) Where a toll order does not authorise a special road authority to assign their rights under the order to charge and to collect tolls, the toll order shall in every case specify the maximum tolls which may be charged for the use of the road or any length of the road in respect of which tolls are charged.

(2) The order may specify different maxima for different descriptions of traffic (which need not correspond with the classes of traffic prescribed by the special road scheme) and may provide for the amounts to be varied in accordance with a formula specified in the order.

(3) Subject to section 32, where a toll order does authorise a special road authority to assign their rights under the order to charge and to collect tolls, it shall not specify any maximum in respect of tolls which may be charged by the concessionaire.

(4) Where a special road authority has authority to assign as described in subsection (3) but no such assignation is made, they shall not charge any tolls in respect of that road unless an extension toll order is made in respect of that road.

32 Toll order in respect of major crossings

(1) A toll order which relates to a road which consists of or includes a major crossing to which there is no reasonably convenient alternative shall specify the maximum tolls which may be charged in respect of that road.

(2) The Secretary of State may make provision by regulations as to what is to be treated as a major crossing for this purpose and as to the circumstances in which another route is to be taken to be, or not to be, a reasonably convenient alternative.

(3) Subject to any such regulations, a major crossing means a crossing of navigable waters more than 100 metres wide and a reasonably convenient alternative means another crossing (other than a ferry) which is free of toll and is within five miles of the crossing in question.

For this purpose—

(a) the width of tidal waters shall be ascertained by reference to the mean high-water mark and the width of other waters by reference to the ordinary limits of the waters, and

(b) the distance between two crossings shall be taken to be the shortest distance between the centre lines of the two crossings.

(4) The order shall specify the maximum tolls which may be charged for the use of the crossing or any length of the road including the crossing; and if the condition as to absence of a reasonably convenient alternative is satisfied in relation to certain types of traffic only, the order shall make provision only in relation to those types of traffic.

If that condition ceases to be satisfied, generally or in relation to certain types of traffic, the provisions of the order as to maximum tolls shall, where an assignation has been granted under section 28(1), cease to apply, or cease to apply to that type of traffic, for so long as that remains the case.

(5) The order may specify different maxima for different descriptions of traffic (which need not correspond with the classes of traffic prescribed by the special road scheme) and may provide for the amounts to be varied in accordance with a formula specified in the order.

(6) Regulations under this section shall be made by statutory instrument and shall not be made unless a draft of them has been laid before and approved by a resolution of each House of Parliament.

Any regulations so made do not apply in relation to an order if notice of the draft order, and of the relevant draft special road scheme, have been published before the regulations come into force.

33 Application of enactments relating to monopolies, &c

(1) For the purposes of—

(a) the Fair Trading Act 1973,

(b) the provisions of the Competition Act 1980 relating to anti-competitive practices, and

(c) the provisions of the Restrictive Trade Practices Act 1976 relating to restrictive agreements,

a person authorised to charge tolls shall be deemed to supply a service, namely, providing the facility to use the road in return for the toll charged.

(2) Where the toll charged is subject to a maximum specified by the toll order, the Fair Trading Act 1973 has effect as if the service deemed by subsection (1) above to be supplied were among those listed in Part I of Schedule 7 to that Act (services excluded from Director's power to make monopoly reference).

(3) The Restrictive Trade Practices Act 1976 has effect in relation to any agreement which—

(a) was made before the date on which this section comes into force, and

(b) becomes subject to registration under that Act on that date by virtue of the effect which an order under section 11 of that Act has as a result of the coming into force of this section,

as if the agreement had become subject to registration by virtue of an order under that section coming into force on that date.

In this subsection "agreement" has the same meaning as in that Act.

34 Variation or revocation of toll order

(1) A toll order may be varied or revoked—

(a) by an order made by the Secretary of State if he made the toll order; and

(b) by an order made by the local roads authority and confirmed by the Secretary of State in any other case.

(2) Without prejudice to section 30 above (extension toll orders), a toll order may not be varied so as to extend the toll period.

(3) A toll order which does not authorise the charging of tolls in respect of the whole length of the special road to which it relates may not be varied so as to extend the length of road in respect of which tolls may be charged.

(4) The Secretary of State may confirm an order made by a local roads authority either without modifications or subject to such modifications as he thinks fit.

(5) Where an assignation has been granted under section 28(1), the toll order may not be varied or revoked without the consent of the concessionaire.

(6) An order under this section may contain such supplementary, incidental and transitional provisions as appear to the roads authority making the order to be necessary or expedient.

(7) The power conferred on the Secretary of State by this section to vary, revoke or confirm an order is exercisable by statutory instrument which shall be subject to annulment in pursuance of a resolution of either House of Parliament; and the provisions of Schedules 1 and 2 to the Roads (Scotland) Act 1984 (procedure in connection with orders) shall not apply to an order under this section.

35 Transfer or termination of assignation

(1) The rights of a concessionaire under an assignation granted under section 28(1) may, with the consent of the special road authority, be assigned by the concessionaire.

(2) Where an assignation granted by the special road authority under section 28(1) terminates or is terminated before the end of the toll period, the authority shall take reasonable steps to grant a fresh assignation to a new concessionaire and the authority may charge and collect tolls in the same way as a concessionaire within the period of two years beginning with that termination but, within that period, only until the earliest, if any, of the following events—

(a) the granting of a fresh assignation;

(b) the expiry of the toll period;

(c) the commencement of an extension toll order.

(3) References in this Part (including this section) to an assignation granted under section 28(1) shall include references to a fresh assignation granted by virtue of subsection (2) above.

(4) An assignation granted under section 28(1) may contain provision as to the circumstances in which, and the extent to which, any sum received by the special road authority—

(a) in consideration for the appointment of a new concessionaire, or

(b) by way of tolls collected by virtue of subsection (2),

is to be applied for the benefit of the former concessionaire or his creditors, as the case may be.

(5) Where an assignation granted by the special road authority under section 28(1) terminates or is terminated before the end of the toll period and the authority either intends to grant a fresh assignation or to charge and collect tolls itself then, for the purposes of the Transfer of Undertakings (Protection of Employment) Regulations 1981, or any regulations replacing those regulations, the concessionaire shall be treated as transferring to the authority an undertaking which, if a new concessionaire is appointed, the authority shall be treated as then transferring to the new concessionaire.

(6) References in this Part to the termination of an assignation are references to the termination of the rights assigned under the assignation.

Further provision with respect to tolls

36 Further provision as to charging of tolls

(1) A toll order may contain provision exempting from liability for tolls such descriptions of traffic as may be specified in the order.

This does not affect the power of the person authorised to charge tolls to grant such other exemptions from toll as he thinks fit.

(2) A toll order shall contain provision exempting from liability to pay any toll—

(a) a police vehicle, identifiable as such by writing or markings on it or otherwise by its appearance, if being used for police purposes;

(b) an ambulance as defined in section 4(2) of the Vehicles (Excise) Act 1971;

(c) a fire engine as so defined;

(d) a vehicle exempt from duty under that Act by virtue of—

section 4(1)(g) of that Act (invalid carriages),

section 4(1)(kb) of that Act (vehicles used for carriage of disabled persons by recognised bodies), or

section 7(2) of that Act (vehicles used by or for purposes of disabled person).

(3) A person authorised to charge tolls may, subject to the provisions of the order—

(a) suspend the collection of tolls;

(b) enter into agreements under which persons compound in advance, on such terms as may be agreed, for the payment of tolls;

(c) charge different tolls according to—

(i) the distance travelled; or

(ii) the day, time of day, week, month or other period; and

(d) charge different tolls for different descriptions of traffic.

In the case of a concessionaire the powers mentioned above are exercisable subject to the provisions of the assignation.

37 Collection of tolls

(1) The Secretary of State may make provision by regulations with respect to the collection of tolls in pursuance of a toll order.

(2) Different provision may be made for different types of road or different types of toll, or for particular roads or particular tolls.

(3) Regulations may, in particular, impose requirements with respect to—

(a) the displaying of lists of tolls, and

(b) the manner of implementing changes in the amount of tolls;

and where any such requirements are imposed, a toll may not be demanded unless they are, or as the case may be have been, complied with.

(4) A person who in respect of the use of a road to which a toll order relates demands a toll—

(a) which he is not authorised to charge, or

(b) which by virtue of subsection (3) may not be demanded,

commits an offence and is liable on summary conviction to a fine not exceeding level 3 on the standard scale.

(5) Regulations under this section shall be made by statutory instrument which shall be subject to annulment in pursuance of a resolution of either House of Parliament.

38 Refusal or failure to pay tolls

(1) A person who without reasonable excuse refuses or fails to pay, or who attempts to evade payment of, a toll which he is liable to pay by virtue of a toll order commits an offence and is liable on summary conviction to a fine not exceeding level 3 on the standard scale.

(2) If it appears to a person employed for the purpose of collecting tolls that a person has, without reasonable excuse, refused or failed to pay a toll which he is liable to pay by virtue of a toll order, he may—

(a) refuse to permit him to pass, or prevent him from passing, through any place at which tolls are payable, and

(b) require him to remove his vehicle from any such place by a particular route, and if he does not comply with such a requirement cause the vehicle to be so removed;

and for the purpose of exercising the powers conferred by this subsection, a person employed for the purpose of the collection of tolls may call upon such assistance as he thinks necessary.

(3) Where a person does not comply with a requirement under subsection (2)(b) as to the removal of his vehicle, he is liable to pay a prescribed charge in respect of the removal of the vehicle.

(4) Where there remains unpaid—

(a) a toll which a person is liable to pay by virtue of a toll order, or

(b) a prescribed charge which he is liable to pay by virtue of subsection (3),

the person authorised to charge tolls may recover from the person liable the amount of the toll or charge together with a reasonable sum to cover administrative expenses.

(5) In this section a "prescribed charge" means such charge as may be specified in, or calculated in accordance with, regulations made by the Secretary of State.

The regulations may provide for the amount of the charge, or any amount used for the purpose of calculating the charge, to be varied in accordance with a formula specified in the regulations.

(6) Regulations under this section shall be made by statutory instrument which shall be subject to annulment in pursuance of a resolution of either House of Parliament.

39 Facilities for collection of tolls

(1) A person authorised to charge tolls may set up and maintain facilities for the collection of tolls.

The consent of the special road authority is required for the setting up of any such facilities by a concessionaire.

(2) Those responsible for the design and construction of facilities for the collection of tolls, and those responsible for the collection of tolls at such facilities, shall have due regard to the need to avoid delaying the passage of such vehicles as are mentioned in section 36(2)(a), (b) or (c) (police vehicles, ambulances and fire engines).

(3) The power of the special road authority under section 104(3)(c) of the Roads (Scotland) Act 1984 to acquire land for the provision of buildings or facilities to be used in connection with the use of the special road includes, in the case of a road subject to a toll order, power to acquire any land required for the purpose of setting up facilities for the collection of tolls.

(4) In this section "facilities for the collection of tolls" means such buildings, structures or other facilities within the boundary of the road, or on land adjoining the road, as are reasonably required for the purpose of or in connection with the collection of tolls in pursuance of a toll order.

40 Restriction of access to toll roads

(1) Where a toll order is in force in relation to a road, no road or private means of access to land shall be so constructed as to afford access to the road except with the consent of the special road authority and, where an assignation has been granted under section 28(1), the concessionaire.

(2) Subsection (1) does not apply to the construction of a road or private means of access by or on behalf of a government department or Minister of the Crown which the department or Minister is satisfied is reasonably required for discharging any function of the department or Minister.

Report

41 Report on toll roads and toll orders in Scotland

(1) In any calendar year in which there occurs an event to which this section applies, the Secretary of State shall in respect of that year lay before Parliament a report informing Parliament of that occurrence or, as the case may be, the number of such occurrences.

(2) This section applies to the following events—

(a) the Secretary of State enters into a contract for the design and construction of a road which is to be subject to a toll order;

(b) there is opened to public use a new road subject to a toll order for which he is the roads authority;

(c) a toll order, or an order varying or revoking a toll order, is made or confirmed by him.

(3) A report under this section shall contain such information as appears to him to be appropriate with respect to the toll orders (whenever made) which are in force during that year or any part of it.

(4) A report under this section shall be laid on or before 31st July in the following calendar year.

Supplementary provisions

42 Environmental assessment of projects involving special roads

(1) In section 20A of the Roads (Scotland) Act 1984 (environmental assessment of certain road construction projects), after subsection (2) (cases in which environmental statement must be published) insert—

"(2A) Any project for the construction of a special road which falls within Annex II to the Directive shall be treated as having such characteristics that it should be made subject to an environmental assessment in accordance with the Directive.".

(2) In section 55A of that Act (environmental assessment of certain road improvement projects), in subsection (2) (cases in which environmental statement must be published) after the word "and" there shall be inserted the words "either the project is in respect of a special road or the project".

43 Provisions as to traffic regulation

(1) The following provisions have effect with respect to the operation of the Road Traffic Regulation Act 1984 ("the 1984 Act") in relation to a road in respect of which an assignation has been granted under section 28(1).

(2) The traffic authority shall consult the concessionaire before making any regulations or order under the 1984 Act specifically relating to the road.

(3) The concessionaire may cause or permit traffic signs (within the meaning of section 64(1) of the 1984 Act) to be placed on or near the road, but subject to any directions given by the traffic authority.

If the concessionaire fails to comply with a direction of the traffic authority as to the placing of traffic signs, the authority may themselves carry out the work required and recover from the concessionaire the expenses reasonably incurred by them in doing so.

(4) The concessionaire may issue a notice under section 14 of the 1984 Act (temporary restriction or prohibition of traffic) having the same effect as a notice issued under that section by the traffic authority.

The Secretary of State may by regulations make provision excluding in relation to such a notice issued by a concessionaire the provisions of the 1984 Act relating to—

(a) the procedure in connection with the issue of the notice,

(b) the maximum duration of the notice, and

(c) the making of provision in relation to alternative roads,

and making instead such other provision as appears to him to be appropriate.

(5) A notice issued by the concessionaire by virtue of subsection (4) may be revoked or varied by the traffic authority and shall cease to have effect if provision inconsistent with it is made by that authority by order or notice under section 14 of the 1984 Act.

(6) Regulations under this section shall be made by statutory instrument which shall be subject to annulment in pursuance of a resolution of either House of Parliament.

44 Exercise of road traffic regulation powers

In Part X of the Road Traffic Regulation Act 1984 (general and supplementary provisions), after section 122 insert—

"122A Prospective exercise of powers

(1) Any power under this Act to make an order or give a direction may be exercised before the road to which it relates is open for public use, so as to take effect immediately on the road's becoming open for public use.

(2) The procedure for making an order or giving a direction applies in such a case with such modifications as may be prescribed.".

45 Classification of traffic for purposes of special roads

In section 8 of the Roads (Scotland) Act 1984 (classification of traffic for purposes of special roads), in subsection (3) there shall be omitted the words from "and where" to the end (which relate to the effect of a variation order on existing schemes) and after that subsection there shall be inserted—

"(4) A variation order may contain provision applying the variations made by the order to existing schemes (whether made by the Secretary of State or a local roads authority); and in the absence of such provision a variation order does not affect the classes of traffic prescribed in an existing scheme.

(5) In subsection (4) above an "existing scheme" means a scheme under section 7 made before the order comes into operation.".

46 Special roads not necessarily to be trunk roads

In section 10 of the Roads (Scotland) Act 1984 (under which a special road provided by the Secretary of State becomes a trunk road), after subsection (2) there shall be inserted—

"(3) Subsections (1) and (2) above shall have effect subject to any provision of the scheme under section 7 of this Act directing that the special road in question or any part of it shall not be a trunk road; but any such provision shall not affect the power of the Secretary of State to make an order under section 5(2)(a) of this Act with respect to the special road or part.".

47 The Roads (Scotland) Act 1984 and the interpretation of Part II

(1) In this Part—

"extension toll order" means a toll order made under section 30(1) authorising the charging of tolls for a new toll period;

"roads authority", "local roads authority" and "special road authority" have the same meaning as in the Roads (Scotland) Act 1984;

"special road" has the same meaning as in that Act;

"special road scheme" means a scheme under section 7 of that Act authorising the provision of a special road;

"toll order" means an order under section 27 authorising the charging of tolls;

"toll period" has the meaning given in section 29(1).

(2) The following provisions of the Roads (Scotland) Act 1984 apply for the purposes of this Part as if it were a part of that Act—

sections 136 to 138 (provisions as to notices), and

section 139 (inquiries).

(3) Where an assignation is granted jointly under section 28(1) by two or more local roads authorities references in this Part to the roads authority shall be construed—

(a) as references to each of those authorities in relation to times, circumstances and purposes before the special road scheme becomes operative, and

(b) in relation to times, circumstances and purposes after the special road scheme becomes operative, as references to the authority which in accordance with the scheme is the special road authority.

(4) Nothing in this Part shall be construed as restricting the powers of a roads authority with respect to a road subject to a toll order in respect of which an assignation has been granted under section 28(1)—

(a) as to the matters which may be provided for in the assignation or as to the making of agreements of any other description for any purpose connected with the special road, or

(b) as to the acquisition, by agreement or compulsorily, of any land which in the opinion of the authority is required, in connection with the road, for any purpose for which the authority may acquire land under Part IX of the Roads (Scotland) Act 1984.

PART III

STREET WORKS IN ENGLAND AND WALES

Introductory provisions

48 Streets, street works and undertakers

(1) In this Part a "street" means the whole or any part of any of the following, irrespective of whether it is a thoroughfare—

(a) any highway, road, lane, footway, alley or passage,

(b) any square or court, and

(c) any land laid out as a way whether it is for the time being formed as a way or not.

Where a street passes over a bridge or through a tunnel, references in this Part to the street include that bridge or tunnel.

(2) The provisions of this Part apply to a street which is not a maintainable highway subject to such exceptions and adaptations as may be prescribed.

(3) In this Part "street works" means works of any of the following kinds (other than works for road purposes) executed in a street in pursuance of a statutory right or a street works licence—

(a) placing apparatus, or

(b) inspecting, maintaining, adjusting, repairing, altering or renewing apparatus, changing the position of apparatus or removing it,

or works required for or incidental to any such works (including, in particular, breaking up or opening the street, or any sewer, drain or tunnel under it, or tunnelling or boring under the street).

(4) In this Part "undertaker" in relation to street works means the person by whom the relevant statutory right is exercisable (in the capacity in which it is exercisable by him) or the licensee under the relevant street works licence, as the case may be.

(5) References in this Part to the undertaker in relation to apparatus in a street are to the person entitled, by virtue of a statutory right or a street works licence, to carry out in relation to the apparatus such works as are mentioned in subsection (3); and references to an undertaker having apparatus in the street, or to the undertaker to whom apparatus belongs, shall be construed accordingly.

49 The street authority and other relevant authorities

(1) In this Part "the street authority" in relation to a street means, subject to the following provisions—

(a) if the street is a maintainable highway, the highway authority, and

(b) if the street is not a maintainable highway, the street managers.

(2) In the case of a highway for which the Secretary of State is the highway authority but in relation to which a local highway authority acts as his agent under section 6 of the Highways Act 1980, the local highway authority shall be regarded as the street authority for the purposes of section 53 (the street works register) and sections 54 to 60 (advance notice and co-ordination of works).

(3) Subsection (1)(b) has effect subject to section 87 as regards the application of this Part to prospectively maintainable highways.

(4) In this Part the expression "street managers", used in relation to a street which is not a maintainable highway, means the authority, body or person liable to the public to maintain or repair the street or, if there is none, any authority, body or person having the management or control of the street.

(5) The Secretary of State may by regulations make provision for exempting street managers from provisions of this Part which would otherwise apply to them as the street authority in relation to a street.

(6) References in this Part to the relevant authorities in relation to any works in a street are to the street authority and also—

(a) where the works include the breaking up or opening of a public sewer in the street, the sewer authority;

(b) where the street is carried or crossed by a bridge vested in a transport authority, or crosses or is crossed by any other property held or used for the purposes of a transport authority, that authority; and

(c) where in any other case the street is carried or crossed by a bridge, the bridge authority.

50 Street works licences

(1) The street authority may grant a licence (a "street works licence") permitting a person—

(a) to place, or to retain, apparatus in the street, and

(b) thereafter to inspect, maintain, adjust, repair, alter or renew the apparatus, change its position or remove it,

and to execute for those purposes any works required for or incidental to such works (including, in particular, breaking up or opening the street, or any sewer, drain or tunnel under it, or tunnelling or boring under the street).

(2) A street works licence authorises the licensee to execute the works permitted by the licence without obtaining any consent which would otherwise be required to be given—

(a) by any other relevant authority in its capacity as such, or

(b) by any person in his capacity as the owner of apparatus affected by the works;

but without prejudice to the provisions of this Part as to the making of requirements by any such authority or person or as to the settlement of a plan and section and the execution of the works in accordance with them.

(3) A street works licence does not dispense the licensee from obtaining any other consent, licence or permission which may be required; and it does not authorise the installation of apparatus for the use of which the licence of the Secretary of State is required, unless and until that licence has been granted.

(4) The provisions of Schedule 3 have effect with respect to the grant of street works licences, the attachment of conditions and other matters.

(5) A street works licence may be granted—

(a) to a person on terms permitting or prohibiting its assignment, or

(b) to the owner of land and his successors in title;

and references in this Part to the licensee are to the person for the time being entitled by virtue of the licence to do anything permitted by it.

(6) Any licence, consent, permission or other authority for the execution in a street of any such works as are mentioned in subsection (1) granted or given by the street authority before the commencement of this Part has effect after the commencement of this Part as a street works licence; but subsection (2) does not apply in relation to such a licence.

This applies in particular to licences granted under section 181 of the Highways Act 1980 or any corresponding earlier enactment.

(7) The works referred to in subsection (1) above do not include works for road purposes.

51 Prohibition of unauthorised street works

(1) It is an offence for a person other than the street authority—

(a) to place apparatus in a street, or

(b) to break up or open a street, or a sewer, drain or tunnel under it, or to tunnel or bore under a street, for the purpose of placing, inspecting, maintaining, adjusting, repairing, altering or renewing apparatus, or of changing the position of apparatus or removing it,

otherwise than in pursuance of a statutory right or a street works licence.

(2) A person committing an offence under this section is liable on summary conviction to a fine not exceeding level 3 on the standard scale.

(3) This section does not apply to works for road purposes or to emergency works of any description.

(4) If a person commits an offence under this section, the street authority may—

(a) in the case of an offence under subsection (1)(a), direct him to remove the apparatus in respect of which the offence was committed, and

(b) in any case, direct him to take such steps as appear to them necessary to reinstate the street or any sewer, drain or tunnel under it.

If he fails to comply with the direction, the authority may remove the apparatus or, as the case may be, carry out the necessary works and recover from him the costs reasonably incurred by them in doing so.

52 Emergency works

(1) In this Part "emergency works" means works whose execution at the time when they are executed is required in order to put an end to, or to prevent the occurrence of, circumstances then existing or imminent (or which the person responsible for the works believes on reasonable grounds to be existing or imminent) which are likely to cause danger to persons or property.

(2) Where works comprise items some of which fall within the preceding definition, the expression "emergency works" shall be taken to include such of the items as do not fall within that definition as cannot reasonably be severed from those that do.

(3) Where in any civil or criminal proceedings brought by virtue of any provision of this Part the question arises whether works were emergency works, it is for the person alleging that they were to prove it.

The street works register

53 The street works register

(1) A street authority shall keep a register showing with respect to each street for which they are responsible such information as may be prescribed with respect to the street works, and such other descriptions of works as may be prescribed, executed or proposed to be executed in the street.

(2) The register shall contain such other information, and shall be kept in such form and manner, as may be prescribed.

(3) The authority shall make the register available for inspection, at all reasonable hours and free of charge—

(a) so far as it relates to restricted information, by any person having authority to execute works of any description in the street, or otherwise appearing to the authority to have a sufficient interest, and

(b) so far as it relates to information which is not restricted, by any person.

The Secretary of State may make provision by regulations as to the information which is restricted for the purposes of this subsection.

(4) The Secretary of State may make arrangements for the duties of street authorities under this section to be discharged by means of one or more central registers kept by a person appointed in pursuance of the arrangements.

(5) If such arrangements are made the Secretary of State may require street authorities to participate in and make contributions towards the cost of the arrangements.

(6) The Secretary of State may by regulations make provision with respect to any register kept in pursuance of this section—

(a) requiring the registration of such information as may be prescribed, and

(b) requiring the payment of such fee as may be prescribed in respect of the registration of information of any prescribed description;

and the regulations may contain provision as to the person responsible for securing the registration of the information and the person liable to pay the fee.

Notice and co-ordination of works

54 Advance notice of certain works

(1) In such cases as may be prescribed an undertaker proposing to execute street works shall give the prescribed advance notice of the works to the street authority.

(2) Different periods of notice may be prescribed for different descriptions of works.

(3) The notice shall contain such information as may be prescribed.

(4) After giving advance notice under this section an undertaker shall comply with such requirements as may be prescribed, or imposed by the street authority, as to the providing of information and other procedural steps to be taken for the purpose of co-ordinating the proposed works with other works of any description proposed to be executed in the street.

(5) An undertaker who fails to comply with his duties under this section commits an offence and is liable on summary conviction to a fine not exceeding level 3 on the standard scale.

55 Notice of starting date of works

(1) An undertaker proposing to begin to execute street works involving—

(a) breaking up or opening the street, or any sewer, drain or tunnel under it, or

(b) tunnelling or boring under the street,

shall give not less than 7 working days' notice (or such other notice as may be prescribed) to the street authority, to any other relevant authority and to any other person having apparatus in the street which is likely to be affected by the works.

(2) Different periods of notice may be prescribed for different descriptions of works, and cases may be prescribed in which no notice is required.

(3) The notice shall state the date on which it is proposed to begin the works and shall contain such other information as may be prescribed.

(4) Where notice is required to be given under this section, the works shall not be begun without notice or before the end of the notice period, except with the consent of those to whom notice is required to be given.

(5) An undertaker who begins to execute any works in contravention of this section commits an offence and is liable on summary conviction to a fine not exceeding level 3 on the standard scale.

(6) In proceedings against a person for such an offence it is a defence for him to show that the contravention was attributable—

(a) to his not knowing the position, or not knowing of the existence, of another person's apparatus, or

(b) to his not knowing the identity or address of—

(i) a relevant authority, or

(ii) the person to whom any apparatus belongs,

and that his ignorance was not due to any negligence on his part or to any failure to make inquiries which he ought reasonably to have made.

(7) A notice under this section shall cease to have effect if the works to which it relates are not substantially begun before the end of the period of 7 working days (or such other period as may be prescribed) beginning with the starting date specified in the notice, or such further period as may be allowed by those to whom notice is required to be given.

56 Power to give directions as to timing of street works

(1) If it appears to the street authority—

(a) that proposed street works are likely to cause serious disruption to traffic, and

(b) that the disruption would be avoided or reduced if the works were carried out only at certain times,

the authority may give the undertaker such directions as may be appropriate as to the times when the works may or may not be carried out.

(2) The procedure for giving a direction shall be prescribed by the Secretary of State.

(3) An undertaker who executes works in contravention of a direction under this section commits an offence and is liable on summary conviction to a fine not exceeding level 3 on the standard scale.

(4) The Secretary of State may issue or approve for the purposes of this section a code of practice giving practical guidance as to the exercise by street authorities of the power conferred by this section; and in exercising that power a street authority shall have regard to the code of practice.

57 Notice of emergency works

(1) Nothing in section 54 (advance notice), section 55 (notice of starting date) or section 56 (directions as to timing of works) affects the right of an undertaker to execute emergency works.

(2) An undertaker executing emergency works shall, if the works are of a kind in respect of which notice is required by section 55, give notice as soon as reasonably practicable, and in any event within two hours (or such other period as may be prescribed) of the works being begun, to the persons to whom notice would be required to be given under that section.

(3) The notice shall state his intention or, as the case may be, the fact that he has begun to execute the works and shall contain such other information as may be prescribed.

(4) An undertaker who fails to give notice in accordance with this section commits an offence and is liable on summary conviction to a fine not exceeding level 3 on the standard scale.

(5) In proceedings against a person for such an offence it is a defence for him to show that the contravention was attributable—

(a) to his not knowing the position, or not knowing of the existence, of another person's apparatus, or

(b) to his not knowing the identity or address of—

(i) a relevant authority, or

(ii) the person to whom any apparatus belongs,

and that his ignorance was not due to any negligence on his part or to any failure to make inquiries which he ought reasonably to have made.

58 Restriction on works following substantial road works

(1) Where it is proposed to carry out substantial road works in a highway, the street authority may by notice in accordance with this section restrict the execution of street works during the twelve months following the completion of those works.

For this purpose substantial road works means works for road purposes, or such works together with other works, of such description as may be prescribed.

(2) The notice shall be published in the prescribed manner and shall specify the nature and location of the proposed works, the date (not being less than three months after the notice is published, or first published) on which it is proposed to begin the works, and the extent of the restriction.

(3) A copy of the notice shall be given to each of the following—

(a) where there is a public sewer in the part of the highway to which the restriction relates, to the sewer authority,

(b) where the part of the highway to which the restriction relates is carried or crossed by a bridge vested in a transport authority, or crosses or is crossed by any other property held or used for the purposes of a transport authority, to that authority,

(c) where in any other case the part of the highway to which the restriction relates is carried or crossed by a bridge, to the bridge authority,

(d) any person who has given notice under section 54 (advance notice of certain works) of his intention to execute street works in the part of the highway to which the restriction relates, and

(e) any other person having apparatus in the part of the highway to which the restriction relates;

but a failure to do so does not affect the validity of the restriction imposed by the notice.

(4) A notice ceases to be effective if the works to which it relates are not substantially begun—

(a) on or within one month from the date specified in the notice, or

(b) where street works are in progress on that date in the part of the highway to which the restriction relates, within one month from the completion of those works.

(5) An undertaker shall not in contravention of a restriction imposed by a notice under this section break up or open the part of the highway to which the restriction relates, except—

(a) to execute emergency works,

(b) with the consent of the street authority, or

(c) in such other cases as may be prescribed.

(6) If he does—

(a) he commits an offence and is liable on summary conviction to a fine not exceeding level 3 on the standard scale, and

(b) he is liable to reimburse the street authority any costs reasonably incurred by them in reinstating the highway.

(7) The consent of the street authority under subsection (5)(b) shall not be unreasonably withheld; and any question whether the withholding of consent is unreasonable shall be settled by arbitration.

(8) An undertaker shall be taken not to have failed to fulfil any statutory duty to afford a supply or service if, or to the extent that, his failure is attributable to a restriction imposed by a notice under this section.

59 General duty of street authority to co-ordinate works

(1) A street authority shall use their best endeavours to co-ordinate the execution of works of all kinds (including works for road purposes) in the streets for which they are responsible—

(a) in the interests of safety,

(b) to minimise the inconvenience to persons using the street (having regard, in particular, to the needs of people with a disability), and

(c) to protect the structure of the street and the integrity of apparatus in it.

(2) That duty extends to co-ordination with other street authorities where works in a street for which one authority are responsible affect streets for which other authorities are responsible.

(3) The Secretary of State shall issue or approve for the purposes of this section codes of practice giving practical guidance as to the matters mentioned above; and in discharging their general duty of co-ordination a street authority shall have regard to any such code of practice.

(4) If it appears to the Secretary of State that a street authority are not properly discharging their general duty of co-ordination, he may direct the authority to supply him with such information as he considers necessary to enable him to decide whether that is the case and if so what action to take.

The direction shall specify the information to be provided and the period within which it is to be provided.

(5) If after the end of that period (whether or not the direction has been complied with) it appears to the Secretary of State that the authority are not properly discharging their general duty of co-ordination, he may direct the authority to take such steps as he considers appropriate for the purpose of discharging that duty.

The direction shall specify the steps to be taken and the period within which they are to be taken, and may include a requirement to make a report or periodic reports to the Secretary of State as to what steps have been taken and the results of taking them.

(6) A direction under this section may be varied or revoked by a further direction.

60 General duty of undertakers to co-operate

(1) An undertaker shall as regards the execution of street works use his best endeavours to co-operate with the street authority and with other undertakers—

(a) in the interests of safety,

(b) to minimise the inconvenience to persons using the street (having regard, in particular, to the needs of people with a disability), and

(c) to protect the structure of the street and the integrity of apparatus in it.

(2) The Secretary of State shall issue or approve for the purposes of this section codes of practice giving practical guidance as to the matters mentioned in subsection (1); and—

(a) so far as an undertaker complies with such a code of practice he shall be taken to comply with his duty under that subsection, and

(b) a failure in any respect to comply with any such code is evidence of failure in that respect to comply with that duty.

(3) An undertaker who fails to comply with his duty under subsection (1) commits an offence and is liable on summary conviction to a fine not exceeding level 3 on the standard scale.

Streets subject to special controls

61 Protected streets

(1) The consent of the street authority is required for the placing of apparatus by an undertaker in a protected street, except as mentioned below.

The following are "protected streets" for this purpose—

(a) any highway or proposed highway which is a special road in accordance with section 16 of the Highways Act 1980, and

(b) any street designated by the street authority as protected.

(2) Consent is not required for the placing of apparatus—

(a) by way of renewal of existing apparatus, or

(b) in pursuance of a street works licence,

unless, in the latter case, the licence was granted before the street became a protected street.

(3) The street authority may require the payment of—

(a) a reasonable fee in respect of the legal or other expenses incurred in connection with the giving of their consent under this section, and

(b) an annual fee of a reasonable amount for administering the consent;

and any such fee is recoverable from the undertaker.

This shall not be construed as affecting any right of the authority where they own the land on which the street is situated to grant for such consideration as they think fit the right to place anything in, under or over the land.

(4) Where the apparatus is to be placed crossing the protected street and not running along it, the street authority shall not withhold their consent unless there are special reasons for doing so.

(5) Consent to the placing of apparatus in a protected street may be given subject to conditions; and the street authority may agree to contribute to the expenses incurred by the undertaker in complying with the conditions.

(6) Any dispute between a street authority and an undertaker as to the withholding of consent, the imposition of conditions, or the making of contributions shall be settled by arbitration.

(7) An undertaker having a statutory duty to afford a supply or service shall not be regarded as in breach of that duty if, or to the extent that, it is not reasonably practicable to afford a supply or service by reason of anything done by the street authority in exercise of their functions under this section.

62 Supplementary provisions as to designation of protected streets

(1) The Secretary of State may prescribe—

(a) the criteria for designating a street as protected,

(b) the procedure for making or withdrawing such a designation, and

(c) the information to be made available by a street authority as to the streets for the time being so designated by them.

(2) Where a street has been designated as protected the street authority may direct an undertaker to remove or change the position of apparatus placed in the street at a time when it was not so designated.

The authority shall indemnify the undertaker in respect of his reasonable expenses in complying with such a direction.

(3) Where a designation is withdrawn the street authority may give such directions as they consider appropriate as to—

(a) the continuance in force of any conditions subject to which consent was given for the placing of apparatus in the street, and

(b) the continuance of entitlement to any contributions in respect of the expenses of an undertaker in complying with such conditions.

(4) Where a designation is made or withdrawn the street authority may give such directions as they consider appropriate with respect to works in progress in the street when the designation comes into force or ceases to have effect.

(5) Any dispute between a street authority and an undertaker as to the exercise by the authority of their powers under subsection (2), (3) or (4) shall be settled by arbitration.

63 Streets with special engineering difficulties

(1) The provisions of Schedule 4 have effect for requiring the settlement of a plan and section of street works to be executed in a street designated by the street authority as having special engineering difficulties.

(2) The Secretary of State may prescribe—

(a) the criteria for designating a street as having special engineering difficulties,

(b) the procedure for making or withdrawing such a designation, and

(c) the information to be made available by a street authority as to the streets for the time being so designated by them.

(3) Where a local highway authority are asked to designate a street as having special engineering difficulties—

(a) by a transport authority on the ground of the proximity of the street to a structure belonging to, or under the management or control of, the authority, or

(b) by an undertaker having apparatus in the street,

and decline to do so, the transport authority or undertaker may appeal to the Secretary of State who may direct that the street be designated.

(4) The designation of a street as having special engineering difficulties shall not be withdrawn except after consultation with any transport authority or undertaker at whose request the designation was made; and a designation made in pursuance of a direction by the Secretary of State shall not be withdrawn except with his consent.

64 Traffic-sensitive streets

(1) Regulations made for the purposes of section 54, 55 or 57 (notices required to be given in respect of street works) may make special provision in relation to street works in a street designated by the street authority as traffic-sensitive.

(2) The Secretary of State may prescribe—

(a) the criteria for designating a street as traffic-sensitive,

(b) the procedure for making or withdrawing such a designation, and

(c) the information to be made available by a street authority as to the streets for the time being so designated by them.

(3) If it appears to the street authority that the prescribed criteria are met only at certain times or on certain dates, a limited designation may be made accordingly.

In such a case the reference in subsection (1) to the execution of works in a street designated as traffic-sensitive shall be construed as a reference to works so executed at those times or on those dates.

General requirements as to execution of street works

65 Safety measures

(1) An undertaker executing street works shall secure—

(a) that any part of the street which is broken up or open, or is obstructed by plant or materials used or deposited in connection with the works, is adequately guarded and lit, and

(b) that such traffic signs are placed and maintained, and where necessary operated, as are reasonably required for the guidance or direction of persons using the street,

having regard, in particular, to the needs of people with a disability.

(2) In discharging in relation to a highway his duty with respect to the placing, maintenance or operation of traffic signs, an undertaker shall comply with any directions given by the traffic authority.

The power of the traffic authority to give directions under this subsection is exercisable subject to any directions given by the Secretary of State under section 65 of the Road Traffic Regulation Act 1984.

(3) The Secretary of State may issue or approve for the purposes of this section codes of practice giving practical guidance as to the matters mentioned in subsection (1); and—

(a) so far as an undertaker complies with such a code of practice he shall be taken to comply with that subsection; and

(b) a failure in any respect to comply with any such code is evidence of failure in that respect to comply with that subsection.

(4) An undertaker who fails to comply with subsection (1) or (2) commits an offence and is liable on summary conviction to a fine not exceeding level 3 on the standard scale.

(5) If it appears to the street authority that an undertaker has failed to comply with subsection (1) or (2), they may take such steps as appear to them necessary and may recover from the undertaker the costs reasonably incurred by them in doing so.

(6) If a person without lawful authority or excuse—

(a) takes down, alters or removes any fence, barrier, traffic sign or light erected or placed in pursuance of subsection (1) or (2) above, or

(b) extinguishes a light so placed,

he commits an offence and is liable on summary conviction to a fine not exceeding level 3 on the standard scale.

66 Avoidance of unnecessary delay or obstruction

(1) An undertaker executing street works which involve—

(a) breaking up or opening the street, or any sewer, drain or tunnel under it, or

(b) tunnelling or boring under the street,

shall carry on and complete the works with all such dispatch as is reasonably practicable.

(2) An undertaker who fails to do so commits an offence and is liable on summary conviction to a fine not exceeding level 3 on the standard scale.

(3) Where an undertaker executing any street works creates an obstruction in a street to a greater extent or for a longer period than is reasonably necessary, the street authority may by notice require him to take such reasonable steps as are specified in the notice to mitigate or discontinue the obstruction.

(4) If the undertaker fails to comply with such a notice within 24 hours of receiving it, or any longer period specified in the notice, the authority may take the necessary steps and recover from him the costs reasonably incurred by them in doing so.

67 Qualifications of supervisors and operatives

(1) It is the duty of an undertaker executing street works involving—

(a) breaking up the street, or any sewer, drain or tunnel under it, or

(b) tunnelling or boring under the street,

to secure that, except in such cases as may be prescribed, the execution of the works is supervised by a person having a prescribed qualification as a supervisor.

(2) It is the duty of an undertaker executing street works involving—

(a) breaking up or opening the street, or any sewer, drain or tunnel under it, or

(b) tunnelling or boring under the street,

to secure that, except in such cases as may be prescribed, there is on site at all times when any such works are in progress at least one person having a prescribed qualification as a trained operative.

(3) An undertaker who fails to comply with his duty under subsection (1) or (2) commits an offence and is liable on summary conviction to a fine not exceeding level 3 on the standard scale.

(4) Regulations made by the Secretary of State for the purposes of this section may include provision with respect to—

(a) the approval of bodies conferring qualifications (and the withdrawal of such approval), and

(b) the circumstances in which a qualification may be conferred.

68 Facilities to be afforded to street authority

(1) An undertaker executing street works shall afford the street authority reasonable facilities for ascertaining whether he is complying with his duties under this Part.

(2) An undertaker who fails to afford the street authority such facilities commits an offence in respect of each failure and is liable on summary conviction to a fine not exceeding level 3 on the standard scale.

69 Works likely to affect other apparatus in the street

(1) Where street works are likely to affect another person's apparatus in the street, the undertaker executing the works shall take all reasonably practicable steps—

(a) to give the person to whom the apparatus belongs reasonable facilities for monitoring the execution of the works, and

(b) to comply with any requirement made by him which is reasonably necessary for the protection of the apparatus or for securing access to it.

(2) An undertaker who fails to comply with subsection (1) commits an offence in respect of each failure and is liable on summary conviction to a fine not exceeding level 3 on the standard scale.

(3) In proceedings against a person for such an offence it is a defence for him to show that the failure was attributable—

(a) to his not knowing the position, or not knowing of the existence, of another person's apparatus, or

(b) to his not knowing the identity or address of the person to whom any apparatus belongs,

and that his ignorance was not due to any negligence on his part or to any failure to make inquiries which he ought reasonably to have made.

Reinstatement

70 Duty of undertaker to reinstate

(1) It is the duty of the undertaker by whom street works are executed to reinstate the street.

(2) He shall begin the reinstatement as soon after the completion of any part of the street works as is reasonably practicable and shall carry on and complete the reinstatement with all such dispatch as is reasonably practicable.

(3) He shall before the end of the next working day after the day on which the reinstatement is completed inform the street authority that he has completed the reinstatement of the street, stating whether the reinstatement is permanent or interim.

(4) If it is interim, he shall complete the permanent reinstatement of the street as soon as reasonably practicable and in any event within six months (or such other period as may be prescribed) from the date on which the interim reinstatement was completed; and he shall notify the street authority when he has done so.

(5) The permanent reinstatement of the street shall include, in particular, the reinstatement of features designed to assist people with a disability.

(6) An undertaker who fails to comply with any provision of this section commits an offence and is liable on summary conviction to a fine not exceeding level 3 on the standard scale.

(7) In proceedings against a person for an offence of failing to comply with subsection (2) it is a defence for him to show that any delay in reinstating the street was in order to avoid hindering the execution of other works, or other parts of the same works, to be undertaken immediately or shortly thereafter.

71 Materials, workmanship and standard of reinstatement

(1) An undertaker executing street works shall in reinstating the street comply with such requirements as may be prescribed as to the specification of materials to be used and the standards of workmanship to be observed.

(2) He shall also ensure that the reinstatement conforms to such performance standards as may be prescribed—

(a) in the case of interim reinstatement, until permanent reinstatement is effected, and

(b) in the case of permanent reinstatement, for the prescribed period after the completion of the reinstatement.

This obligation is extended in certain cases and restricted in others by the provisions of section 73 as to cases where a reinstatement is affected by subsequent works.

(3) Regulations made for the purposes of this section may make different provision in relation to different classes of excavation and different descriptions of street, and in relation to interim and permanent reinstatement.

(4) The Secretary of State may issue or approve for the purposes of this section codes of practice giving practical guidance as to the matters mentioned in subsections (1) and (2); and regulations made for the purposes of this section may provide that—

(a) so far as an undertaker complies with such a code of practice he shall be taken to comply with his duties under this section; and

(b) a failure in any respect to comply with any such code is evidence of failure in that respect to comply with those duties.

(5) An undertaker who fails to comply with his duties under this section commits an offence and is liable on summary conviction to a fine not exceeding level 3 on the standard scale.

72 Powers of street authority in relation to reinstatement

(1) The street authority may carry out such investigatory works as appear to them to be necessary to ascertain whether an undertaker has complied with his duties under this Part with respect to reinstatement.

If such a failure is disclosed, the undertaker shall bear the cost of the investigatory works; if not, the street authority shall bear the cost of the investigatory works and of any necessary reinstatement.

(2) Where an undertaker has failed to comply with his duties under this Part with respect to reinstatement, he shall bear the cost of—

(a) a joint inspection with the street authority to determine the nature of the failure and what remedial works need to be undertaken,

(b) an inspection by the authority of the remedial works in progress, and

(c) an inspection by the authority when the remedial works have been completed.

(3) The street authority may by notice require an undertaker who has failed to comply with his duties under this Part with respect to reinstatement to carry out the necessary remedial works within such period of not less than 7 working days as may be specified in the notice.

If he fails to comply with the notice, the authority may carry out the necessary works and recover from him the costs reasonably incurred by them in doing so.

(4) If it appears to the street authority that a failure by an undertaker to comply with his duties under this Part as to reinstatement is causing danger to users of the street, the authority may carry out the necessary works without first giving notice and may recover from him the costs reasonably incurred by them in doing so.

They shall, however, give notice to him as soon as reasonably practicable stating their reasons for taking immediate action.

73 Reinstatement affected by subsequent works

(1) The provisions of this section apply in relation to an undertaker's duty under section 71(2) to ensure that a reinstatement conforms to the prescribed performance standards for the requisite period; and references to responsibility for a reinstatement and to the period of that responsibility shall be construed accordingly.

(2) Where a reinstatement is affected by remedial works executed by the undertaker in order to comply with his duties under this Part with respect to reinstatement and the extent of the works exceeds that prescribed, the subsequent reinstatement shall be treated as a new reinstatement as regards the period of his responsibility.

(3) Where the street authority carry out investigatory works in pursuance of section 72(1) and the investigation does not disclose any failure by the undertaker to comply with his duties under this Part with respect to reinstatement, then, to the extent that the original reinstatement has been disturbed by the investigatory works, the responsibility of the undertaker for the reinstatement shall cease.

(4) Where a reinstatement is affected by remedial works executed by the street authority in exercise of their powers under section 72(3) or (4) (powers to act in default of undertaker)—

(a) the undertaker is responsible for the subsequent reinstatement carried out by the authority, and

(b) if the extent of the works exceeds that prescribed, the subsequent reinstatement shall be treated as a new reinstatement as regards the period of his responsibility.

(5) The following provisions apply where a reinstatement is affected by subsequent works in the street otherwise than as mentioned above.

(6) If the reinstatement is dug out to any extent in the course of the subsequent works, the responsibility of the undertaker for the reinstatement shall cease to that extent.

(7) If in any other case the reinstatement ceases to conform to the prescribed performance standards by reason of the subsequent works, the responsibility of the undertaker for the reinstatement is transferred to the person executing the subsequent works; and the provisions of this Part apply in relation to him as they would have applied in relation to the undertaker.

(8) Where there are successive subsequent works affecting a reinstatement, then as between earlier and later works—

(a) subsections (6) and (7) apply in relation to the cessation or transfer of the responsibility of the person for the time being responsible for the reinstatement; and

(b) if the reinstatement ceases to conform to the prescribed performance standards by reason of the works or any of them, it shall be presumed until the contrary is proved that this was caused by the later or last of the works.

Charges, fees and contributions payable by undertakers

74 Charge for occupation of the highway where works unreasonably prolonged

(1) The Secretary of State may make provision by regulations requiring an undertaker executing street works in a maintainable highway to pay a charge to the highway authority where—

(a) the duration of the works exceeds such period as may be prescribed, and

(b) the works are not completed within a reasonable period.

(2) For this purpose "a reasonable period" means such period as is agreed by the authority and the undertaker to be reasonable or, in default of such agreement, is determined by arbitration to be reasonable, for completion of the works in question.

In default of agreement, the authority's view as to what is a reasonable period shall be acted upon pending the decision of the arbitrator.

(3) The regulations may provide that if an undertaker has reason to believe that the duration of works will exceed the prescribed period he may submit to the authority an estimate of their likely duration—

(a) in the case of works in connection with the initial placing of apparatus in the street in pursuance of a street works licence, together with his application for the licence,

(b) in the case of other works (not being emergency works), together with his notice under section 55 (notice of starting date), or

(c) in the case of emergency works, as soon as reasonably practicable after the works are begun,

and that the period stated in an estimate so submitted shall be taken to be agreed by the authority to be reasonable unless they give notice, in such manner and within such period as may be prescribed, objecting to the estimate.

(4) The regulations may also provide that if it appears to the undertaker that by reason of matters not previously foreseen or reasonably foreseeable the duration of the works—

(a) is likely to exceed the prescribed period,

(b) is likely to exceed the period stated in his previous estimate, or

(c) is likely to exceed the period previously agreed or determined to be a reasonable period,

he may submit an estimate or revised estimate accordingly, and that if he does so any previous estimate, agreement or determination shall cease to have effect and the period stated in the new estimate shall be taken to be agreed by the authority to be reasonable unless they give notice, in such manner and within such period as may be prescribed, objecting to the estimate.

(5) The amount of the charge shall be determined in such manner as may be prescribed by reference to the time taken to complete the works and the extent to which the surface of the highway is affected by the works.

Different rates of charge may be prescribed according to the place and time at which the works are executed and such other factors as appear to the Secretary of State to be relevant.

(6) The regulations may make provision as to the time and manner of making payment of any charge.

(7) The regulations shall provide that a highway authority may reduce the amount, or waive payment, of a charge in any particular case, in such classes of case as they may decide or as may be prescribed, or generally.

(8) The first regulations for the purposes of this section shall not be made unless a draft of them has been laid before and approved by a resolution of each House of Parliament; subsequent regulations shall be subject to annulment in pursuance of a resolution of either House of Parliament.

75 Inspection fees

(1) An undertaker executing street works shall, subject to the provisions of any scheme under this section, pay to the street authority the prescribed fee in respect of each inspection of the works carried out by the authority.

(2) Different fees may be prescribed according to the nature or extent of the excavation or other works, the place where they are executed and such other factors as appear to the Secretary of State to be relevant.

(3) The Secretary of State may by regulations make a scheme under which undertakers pay the prescribed fee only in respect of such proportion or number of excavations or other works as may be determined in accordance with the scheme.

(4) The scheme may make provision—

(a) as to the periods and areas by reference to which the proportion or number is to be determined, and

(b) as to the intervals at which an account is to be struck between an undertaker and a street authority and any necessary payment or repayment made;

and different provision may be made for different descriptions of undertaker and different descriptions of street authority.

(5) Nothing in this section applies in relation to inspections in respect of which the undertaker is obliged to bear the cost under section 72(2) (inspections consequent on his failure to comply with his duties as to reinstatement).

76 Liability for cost of temporary traffic regulation

(1) Where by reason of street works—

(a) the traffic authority makes an order or issues a notice under section 14 of the Road Traffic Regulation Act 1984 (temporary prohibition or restriction of traffic), or

(b) a concessionaire issues a notice under that section by virtue of section 3(4) of this Act,

the authority or concessionaire may recover from the undertaker the whole of the costs incurred by them in connection with or in consequence of the order or notice.

(2) Those costs shall be taken to include, in particular, the cost to the authority or concessionaire—

(a) of complying with any requirement to notify the public of any matter in connection with the making, issuing or operation of the order or notice, and

(b) of providing traffic signs in connection with the prohibition or restriction of traffic by the order or notice.

77 Liability for cost of use of alternative route

(1) Where by reason of street works the use of a highway is restricted or prohibited and the diverted traffic uses as an alternative route a highway of a lower classification, the undertaker shall indemnify the highway authority for the latter highway in respect of costs reasonably incurred by them—

(a) in strengthening the highway, so far as that is done with a view to and is necessary for the purposes of its use by the diverted traffic; or

(b) in making good any damage to the highway occurring in consequence of the use by it of the diverted traffic.

(2) For this purpose the order of classification of highways, from higher to lower, is as follows:

1	Trunk roads.
2	Principal roads.
3	Other classified roads.
4	Other highways.

As to principal and other classified roads, see sections 12 and 13 of the Highways Act 1980.

78 Contributions to costs of making good long-term damage

(1) The Secretary of State may make provision by regulations requiring an undertaker executing street works to contribute to the costs incurred or likely to be incurred by the street authority or, in the case of a road subject to a concession within the meaning of Part I of this Act, by the concessionaire, in works of reconstruction or re-surfacing of the street.

(2) The regulations may provide—

(a) for a contribution to the cost of particular remedial works, or

(b) for a general contribution calculated in such manner as may be prescribed.

(3) In the former case the regulations may contain provision for apportioning the liability where the need for the remedial works is attributable to works executed by more than one person.

(4) In the latter case the regulations may provide for the amount of the contribution to vary according to the nature of the street, the description and extent of the works and such other factors as appear to the Secretary of State to be relevant.

(5) The first regulations under this section shall not be made unless a draft of them has been laid before and approved by a resolution of each House of Parliament; subsequent regulations shall be subject to annulment in pursuance of a resolution of either House of Parliament.

Duties and liabilities of undertakers with respect to apparatus

79 Records of location of apparatus

(1) An undertaker shall, except in such cases as may be prescribed, record the location of every item of apparatus belonging to him as soon as reasonably practicable after—

(a) placing it in the street or altering its position,

(b) locating it in the street in the course of executing any other works, or

(c) being informed of its location under section 80 below,

stating the nature of the apparatus and (if known) whether it is for the time being in use.

(2) The records shall be kept up to date and shall be kept in such form and manner as may be prescribed.

(3) An undertaker shall make his records available for inspection, at all reasonable hours and free of charge, by any person having authority to execute works of any description in the street or otherwise appearing to the undertaker to have a sufficient interest.

(4) If an undertaker fails to comply with his duties under this section—

(a) he commits an offence and is liable on summary conviction to a fine not exceeding level 3 on the standard scale; and

(b) he is liable to compensate any person in respect of damage or loss incurred by him in consequence of the failure.

(5) In criminal or civil proceedings arising out of any such failure it is a defence for the undertaker to show that all reasonable care was taken by him, and by his contractors and by persons in his employ or that of his contractors, to secure that no such failure occurred.

(6) An order under section 102 (power to make consequential amendments, repeals, &c.) relating to an enactment or instrument containing provision for the keeping of records of apparatus which appears to the Secretary of State to be superseded by or otherwise inconsistent with the provisions of this section—

(a) shall not be subject to the procedure provided for in Schedule 5, and

(b) may make such transitional and other provision as appears to the Secretary of State appropriate for applying in relation to records compiled under that enactment or instrument the provisions of subsections (2) to (5) above and section 80 below.

80 Duty to inform undertakers of location of apparatus

(1) A person executing works of any description in the street who finds apparatus belonging to an undertaker which is not marked, or is wrongly marked, on the records made available by the undertaker, shall take such steps as are reasonably practicable to inform the undertaker to whom the apparatus belongs of its location and (so far as appears from external inspection) its nature and whether it is in use.

(2) Where a person executing works of any description in the street finds apparatus which does not belong to him and is unable, after taking such steps as are reasonably practicable, to ascertain to whom the apparatus belongs, he shall—

- (a) if he is an undertaker, note on the records kept by him under section 79(1) (in such manner as may be prescribed) the location of the apparatus he has found and its general description; and
- (b) in any other case, inform the street authority of the location and general description of the apparatus he has found.

(3) Subsections (1) and (2) have effect subject to such exceptions as may be prescribed.

(4) A person who fails to comply with subsection (1) or (2) commits an offence and is liable on summary conviction to a fine not exceeding level 3 on the standard scale.

81 Duty to maintain apparatus

(1) An undertaker having apparatus in the street shall secure that the apparatus is maintained to the reasonable satisfaction of—

- (a) the street authority, as regards the safety and convenience of persons using the street (having regard, in particular, to the needs of people with a disability), the structure of the street and the integrity of apparatus of the authority in the street, and
- (b) any other relevant authority, as regards any land, structure or apparatus of theirs;

and he shall afford reasonable facilities to each such authority for ascertaining whether it is so maintained.

(2) For this purpose maintenance means the carrying out of such works as are necessary to keep the apparatus in efficient working condition (including periodic renewal where appropriate); and includes works rendered necessary by other works in the street, other than major highway, bridge or transport works (as to which, see sections 84 and 85 below).

(3) If an undertaker fails to give a relevant authority the facilities required by this section—

- (a) the street authority may in such cases as may be prescribed, and
- (b) any other relevant authority may in any case,

execute such works as are needed to enable them to inspect the apparatus in question, including any necessary breaking up or opening of the street.

(4) If an undertaker fails to secure that apparatus is maintained to the reasonable satisfaction of a relevant authority in accordance with this section—

- (a) the street authority may in such cases as may be prescribed, and
- (b) any other relevant authority may in any case,

execute any emergency works needed in consequence of the failure.

(5) The provisions of this Part apply in relation to works executed by a relevant authority under subsection (3) or (4) as if they were executed by the undertaker; and the undertaker shall indemnify the authority in respect of the costs reasonably incurred by them in executing the works.

(6) A relevant authority who execute or propose to execute any works under subsection (3) or (4) shall give notice to any other relevant authority as soon as reasonably practicable stating the general nature of the works.

(7) Nothing in subsection (3) or (4) shall be construed as excluding any other means of securing compliance with the duties imposed by subsection (1).

82 Liability for damage or loss caused

(1) An undertaker shall compensate—

- (a) the street authority or any other relevant authority in respect of any damage or loss suffered by the authority in their capacity as such, and
- (b) any other person having apparatus in the street in respect of any expense reasonably incurred in making good damage to that apparatus,

as a result of the execution by the undertaker of street works or any event of a kind mentioned in subsection (2).

(2) The events referred to in subsection (1) are any explosion, ignition, discharge or other event occurring to gas, electricity, water or any other thing required for the purposes of a supply or service afforded by an undertaker which—

- (a) at the time of or immediately before the event in question was in apparatus of the undertaker in the street, or
- (b) had been in such apparatus before that event and had escaped therefrom in circumstances which contributed to its occurrence.

(3) The liability of an undertaker under this section arises—

- (a) whether or not the damage or loss is attributable to negligence on his part or on the part of any person for whom he is responsible, and
- (b) notwithstanding that he is acting in pursuance of a statutory duty.

(4) However, his liability under this section does not extend to damage or loss which is attributable to misconduct or negligence on the part of—

- (a) the person suffering the damage or loss, or any person for whom he is responsible, or
- (b) a third party, that is, a person for whom neither the undertaker nor the person suffering the damage or loss is responsible.

(5) For the purposes of this section the persons for whom a person is responsible are his contractors and any person in his employ or that of his contractors.

(6) Nothing in this section shall be taken as exonerating an undertaker from any liability to which he would otherwise be subject.

Apparatus affected by highway, bridge or transport works

83 Works for road purposes likely to affect apparatus in the street

(1) This section applies to works for road purposes other than major highway works (as to which see section 84 below).

(2) Where works to which this section applies are likely to affect apparatus in the street, the authority executing the works shall take all reasonably practicable steps—

(a) to give the person to whom the apparatus belongs reasonable facilities for monitoring the execution of the works, and

(b) to comply with any requirement made by him which is reasonably necessary for the protection of the apparatus or for securing access to it.

(3) An authority who fail to comply with subsection (2) commit an offence in respect of each failure and are liable on summary conviction to a fine not exceeding level 3 on the standard scale.

(4) In proceedings against an authority for such an offence it is a defence for them to show that the failure was attributable—

(a) to their not knowing the position, or not knowing of the existence, of a person's apparatus, or

(b) to their not knowing the identity or address of the person to whom any apparatus belongs,

and that their ignorance was not due to any negligence on their part or to any failure to make inquiries which they ought reasonably to have made.

84 Measures necessary where apparatus affected by major works

(1) Where an undertaker's apparatus in a street is or may be affected by major highway works, major bridge works or major transport works, the highway, bridge or transport authority concerned and the undertaker shall take such steps as are reasonably required—

(a) to identify any measures needing to be taken in relation to the apparatus in consequence of, or in order to facilitate, the execution of the authority's works,

(b) to settle a specification of the necessary measures and determine by whom they are to be taken, and

(c) to co-ordinate the taking of those measures and the execution of the authority's works,

so as to secure the efficient implementation of the necessary work and the avoidance of unnecessary delay.

(2) The Secretary of State may issue or approve for the purposes of this section a code of practice giving practical guidance as to the matters mentioned in subsection (1) and the steps to be taken by the authority and the undertaker.

(3) Any dispute between the authority and the undertaker as to any of the matters mentioned in subsection (1) shall, in default of agreement, be settled by arbitration.

(4) If the authority or the undertaker fails to comply with an agreement between them as to any of those matters, or with the decision of the arbitrator under subsection (3), the authority or undertaker shall be liable to compensate the other in respect of any loss or damage resulting from the failure.

85 Sharing of cost of necessary measures

(1) Where an undertaker's apparatus in a street is affected by major highway works, major bridge works or major transport works, the allowable costs of the measures needing to be taken in relation to the apparatus in consequence of the works, or in order to facilitate their execution, shall be borne by the highway, bridge or transport authority concerned and the undertaker in such manner as may be prescribed.

(2) The regulations may make provision as to the costs allowable for this purpose.

Provision may, in particular, be made for disallowing costs of the undertaker—

(a) where the apparatus in question was placed in the street after the authority had given the undertaker the prescribed notice of their intention to execute the works, or

(b) in respect of measures taken to remedy matters for which the authority were not to blame,

and for allowing only such costs of either party as are not recoverable from a third party.

(3) Where the authority have a right to recover from a third party their costs in taking measures in relation to undertaker's apparatus but in accordance with section 84 it is determined that the measures should be taken by the undertaker, the right of the authority includes a right to recover the undertaker's costs in taking those measures and they shall account to the undertaker for any sum received.

(4) The regulations shall provide for the allowable costs to be borne by the authority and the undertaker in such proportions as may be prescribed.

Different proportions may be prescribed for different cases or classes of case.

(5) The regulations may require the undertaker to give credit for any financial benefit to him from the betterment or deferment of renewal of the apparatus resulting from the measures taken.

(6) The regulations may make provision as to the time and manner of making any payment required under this section.

Provisions with respect to particular authorities and undertakings

86 Highway authorities, highways and related matters

(1) In this Part—

"highway authority" and "local highway authority" have the same meaning as in the Highways Act 1980; and

"maintainable highway" means a highway which for the purposes of that Act is maintainable at the public expense.

(2) In this Part "works for road purposes" means works of any of the following descriptions executed in relation to a highway—

(a) works for the maintenance of the highway,

(b) any works under powers conferred by Part V of the Highways Act 1980 (improvement),

(c) the erection, maintenance, alteration or removal of traffic signs on or near the highway, or

(d) the construction of a crossing for vehicles across a footway or grass verge or the strengthening or adaptation of a footway for use as a crossing for vehicles,

or works of any corresponding description executed in relation to a street which is not a highway.

(3) In this Part "major highway works" means works of any of the following descriptions executed by the highway authority in relation to a highway which consists of or includes a carriageway—

(a) reconstruction or widening of the highway,

(b) works carried out in exercise of the powers conferred by section 64 of the Highways Act 1980 (dual carriageways and roundabouts),

(c) substantial alteration of the level of the highway,

(d) provision, alteration of the position or width, or substantial alteration in the level of a carriageway, footway or cycle track in the highway,

(e) the construction or removal of a road hump within the meaning of section 90F of the Highways Act 1980,

(f) works carried out in exercise of the powers conferred by section 184 of the Highways Act 1980 (vehicle crossings over footways and verges),

(g) provision of a cattle-grid in the highway or works ancillary thereto, or

(h) tunnelling or boring under the highway.

(4) Works executed under section 184(9) of the Highways Act 1980 by a person other than the highway authority shall also be treated for the purposes of this Part as major highway works; and in relation to such works the references in sections 84 and 85 to the highway authority shall be construed as references to him.

87 Prospectively maintainable highways

(1) Where a local highway authority are satisfied that a street in their area (whether a highway or not) is likely to become a maintainable highway, they may make a declaration to that effect.

(2) The declaration shall be a local land charge.

(3) The provisions of this Part apply to a street in respect of which such a declaration has been made and registered as a local land charge as they apply to a maintainable highway.

(4) In relation to street works in such a street, the street authority—

(a) shall secure the performance by undertakers of their duties under this Part, and shall exercise their powers under this Part, in such manner as is reasonably required for the protection of the street managers; and

(b) shall comply with any reasonable request as to securing performance of those duties, or as to the exercise of those powers, which may be made by the street managers.

88 Bridges, bridge authorities and related matters

(1) In this Part—

(a) references to a bridge include so much of any street as gives access to the bridge and any embankment, retaining wall or other work or substance supporting or protecting that part of the street; and

(b) "bridge authority" means the authority, body or person in whom a bridge is vested.

(2) In this Part "major bridge works" means works for the replacement, reconstruction or substantial alteration of a bridge.

(3) Where a street is carried or crossed by a bridge, any statutory right to place apparatus in the street includes the right to place apparatus in, and attach apparatus to, the structure of the bridge; and other rights to execute works in relation to the apparatus extend accordingly.

References in this Part to apparatus in the street include apparatus so placed or attached.

(4) An undertaker proposing to execute street works affecting the structure of a bridge shall consult the bridge authority before giving notice under section 55 (notice of starting date) in relation to the works.

(5) An undertaker executing such works shall take all reasonably practicable steps—

(a) to give the bridge authority reasonable facilities for monitoring the execution of the works, and

(b) to comply with any requirement made by them which is reasonably necessary for the protection of the bridge or for securing access to it.

(6) An undertaker who fails to comply with subsection (4) or (5) commits an offence in respect of each failure and is liable on summary conviction to a fine not exceeding level 3 on the standard scale.

(7) Subsections (4) to (6) do not apply to works in relation to which Schedule 4 applies (works in streets with special engineering difficulties).

89 Public sewers, sewer authorities and related matters

(1) In this Part—

(a) "sewer" and "public sewer" have the same meaning as in the Water Act 1989, and

(b) "sewer authority", in relation to a public sewer, means the sewerage undertaker within the meaning of that Act in whom the sewer is vested.

(2) An undertaker proposing to execute street works affecting a public sewer shall consult the sewer authority before giving notice under section 55 (notice of starting date) in relation to the works.

(3) References in this Part to apparatus include a sewer, drain or tunnel.

(4) References to the undertaker in relation to such apparatus, or in relation to street works in connection with such apparatus, shall be construed—

(a) in the case of a public sewer, as references to the sewer authority, and

(b) in any other case, as references to the authority, body or person having the management or control of the sewer, drain or tunnel.

(5) Section 69 (provisions as to works likely to affect other apparatus in the street) does not apply by virtue of subsection (3) above in relation to works likely to affect a public sewer if, or to the extent that, Schedule 4 (works in streets with special engineering difficulties) applies.

90 Provisions as to reinstatement of sewers, drains or tunnels

(1) The duties of an undertaker under this Part with respect to reinstatement of the street extend, in the case of street works which involve breaking up or opening a sewer, drain or tunnel, to the reinstatement of the sewer, drain or tunnel.

(2) The responsible authority may by notice require an undertaker who has failed to comply with his duties under this Part with respect to reinstatement to carry out the necessary remedial works within such period of not less than 7 working days as may be specified in the notice.

If he fails to comply with the notice, the authority may carry out the necessary works and recover from him the costs reasonably incurred by them in doing so.

(3) If it appears to the responsible authority that a failure by an undertaker to comply with his duties under this Part as to reinstatement is causing danger to users of the street, the authority may carry out the necessary works without first giving notice and may recover from him the costs reasonably incurred by them in doing so.

They shall, however, give notice to him as soon as reasonably practicable stating their reasons for taking immediate action.

(4) The responsible authority for the purposes of this section is—

(a) in the case of a public sewer, the sewer authority, and

(b) in the case of any other sewer, drain or tunnel, the authority, body or person having the management or control of it.

91 Transport authorities, transport undertakings and related matters

(1) In this Part—

(a) "transport authority" means the authority, body or person having the control or management of a transport undertaking; and

(b) "transport undertaking" means a railway, tramway, dock, harbour, pier, canal or inland navigation undertaking of which the activities, or some of the activities, are carried on under statutory authority.

(2) In this Part "major transport works" means substantial works required for the purposes of a transport undertaking and executed in property held or used for the purposes of the undertaking.

(3) References in this Part to a street which crosses or is crossed by property held or used for the purposes of a transport undertaking extend to cases in which the street and the property in question are at different levels.

But the transport authority shall not be treated as a relevant authority as regards undertakers' works in such a street where the property in question consists only of—

(a) subsoil of the street which is held by the transport authority but is not used, and has not been adapted for use, for the purposes of the transport undertaking, or

(b) property underground at such a depth that there is no reasonable possibility of the works affecting it.

(4) The provisions of this Part relating to a street which crosses or is crossed by property held or used for the purposes of a transport undertaking apply to a street which is or forms part of a towing-path or other way running along a canal or inland navigation,

provided the path or way is held or used, or the subsoil of it is held, for the purposes of the canal or inland navigation undertaking.

92 Special precautions as to displaying of lights

(1) An undertaker executing street works in a street which crosses, or is crossed by, or is in the vicinity of, a railway, tramway, dock, harbour, pier, canal or inland navigation, shall comply with any reasonable requirements imposed by the transport authority concerned with respect to the displaying of lights so as to avoid any risk of their—

(a) being mistaken for any signal light or other light used for controlling, directing or securing the safety of traffic thereon, or

(b) being a hindrance to the ready interpretation of any such signal or other light.

(2) An undertaker who fails to comply with any such requirement commits an offence and is liable on summary conviction to a fine not exceeding level 3 on the standard scale.

(3) In proceedings for such an offence it is a defence for the undertaker to show that all reasonable care was taken by him, and by his contractors and by persons in his employ or that of his contractors, to secure that no such failure occurred.

93 Works affecting level crossings or tramways

(1) This section applies to street works at a crossing of a railway on the level or which affect a tramway.

In this section "the relevant transport authority" means the authority having the management of the railway or tramway undertaking concerned.

(2) An undertaker proposing to begin to execute works to which this section applies shall give the prescribed notice to the relevant transport authority notwithstanding that such notice is not required under section 55 (notice of starting date).

The provisions of subsections (2) to (7) of that section (contents of notice, when works may be begun, &c.) apply in relation to the notice required by this subsection as in relation to a notice under subsection (1) of that section.

(3) An undertaker executing works to which this section applies shall comply with any reasonable requirements made by the relevant transport authority—

(a) for securing the safety of persons employed in connection with the works, or

(b) for securing that interference with traffic on the railway or tramway caused by the execution of the works is reduced so far as is practicable;

and, except where submission of a plan and section is required, he shall defer beginning the works for such further period as the relevant transport authority may reasonably request as needed for formulating their requirements under this subsection or making their traffic arrangements.

(4) Nothing in subsection (2) or (3) affects the right of an undertaker to execute emergency works.

(5) An undertaker executing emergency works shall give notice to the relevant transport authority as soon as reasonably practicable of his intention or, as the case may be, of his having begun to do so notwithstanding that such notice is not required by section 57 (notice of emergency works).

The provisions of subsections (3) and (4) of that section (contents of notice and penalty for failure to give notice) apply in relation to the notice required by this subsection as in relation to a notice under subsection (2) of that section.

Power of street authority or district council to undertake street works

94 Power of street authority or district council to undertake street works

(1) A street authority or district council may enter into an agreement with an undertaker for the execution by the authority or council on behalf of the undertaker of any street works.

(2) The agreement may contain such terms as to payment and otherwise as the parties consider appropriate.

(3) Nothing in this section shall be construed as derogating from any powers exercisable by the authority or council apart from this section.

(4) This section shall cease to have effect upon such day as the Secretary of State may appoint by order made by statutory instrument which shall be subject to annulment in pursuance of a resolution of either House of Parliament.

Supplementary provisions

95 Offences

(1) Any provision of this Part imposing criminal liability in respect of any matter is without prejudice to any civil liability in respect of the same matter.

(2) Where a failure to comply with a duty imposed by this Part is continued after conviction, the person in default commits a further offence.

96 Recovery of costs or expenses

(1) Any provision of this Part enabling an authority, body or person to recover the costs or expenses of taking any action shall be taken to include the relevant administrative expenses of that authority, body or person including an appropriate sum in respect of general staff costs and overheads.

The Secretary of State may prescribe the basis on which such amounts are to be calculated; and different provision may be made for different cases or descriptions of case.

(2) Where a right to payment enuring for the benefit of a person is conferred in respect of the same matter—

(a) both under this Part and under any enactment or agreement passed or made before the commencement of this Part, or

(b) by two or more provisions of this Part,

a payment made in discharge of any of those rights shall be treated as being made in or towards satisfaction of the other or others.

(3) Where under any provision of this Part a person is entitled in certain circumstances to recover costs or expenses incurred by him in executing works or taking other steps, any dispute as to the existence of those circumstances or as to the amount recoverable shall be determined by arbitration.

This applies whether the provision is expressed as conferring a right to recover, or as imposing a liability to reimburse or indemnify or to bear the cost, but does not apply in relation to a provision expressed as providing for the charging of a fee or conferring a right to compensation or in relation to section 78 (contributions to cost of making good long-term damage to the street).

97 Service of notices and other documents

(1) Notices required or authorised to be given for the purposes of this Part shall be given in the prescribed form.

(2) The Secretary of State may make provision by regulations as to the manner of service of notices and other documents required or authorised to be served for the purposes of this Part.

98 Reckoning of periods

(1) In reckoning for the purposes of this Part a period expressed as a period from or before a given date, that date shall be excluded.

(2) For the purposes of this Part a working day means a day other than a Saturday, Sunday, Christmas Day, Good Friday or a bank holiday; and a notice given after 4.30 p.m. on a working day shall be treated as given on the next working day.

(3) In subsection (2) a "bank holiday" means a day which is a bank holiday under the Banking and Financial Dealings Act 1971 in the locality in which the street in question is situated.

99 Arbitration

Any matter which under this Part is to be settled by arbitration shall be referred to a single arbitrator appointed by agreement between the parties concerned or, in default of agreement, by the President of the Institution of Civil Engineers.

100 Agreements inconsistent with the provisions of this Part

(1) An agreement which purports to make provision regulating the execution of street works is of no effect to the extent that it is inconsistent with the provisions of this Part.

(2) This does not affect an agreement for the waiver or variation of a right conferred on a relevant authority by any of the provisions of this Part which is made after the right has accrued and is not inconsistent with the future operation of those provisions.

101 Effect of this Part on certain existing special enactments or instruments

(1) Any special enactment passed or made before the commencement of this Part which makes or authorises the making of provision regulating the execution of street works in a manner inconsistent with the provisions of this Part shall cease to have effect;

and unless a contrary intention appears no enactment passed or made after the commencement of this Part shall be construed as making or authorising the making of any such provision.

This subsection does not apply to any provision as to the obtaining of consent for the execution of the works or for any other purpose.

(2) Any special enactment passed or made before the commencement of this Part which requires the consent of a relevant authority (in its capacity as such) to the execution of street works shall cease to have effect, except as mentioned below; and unless a contrary intention appears no special enactment passed or made after the commencement of this Part shall be construed as requiring such consent.

This subsection does not apply to a consent requirement so far as it relates to—

(a) works above the surface of the highway, or

(b) works outside the limits of supply of an undertaker in relation to whom such limits are imposed.

(3) A provision made by way of condition imposed on the giving of a consent for the execution of street works is of no effect in so far as it would have been so by virtue of section 100 if it had been made by an agreement.

(4) If it appears to the Secretary of State—

(a) that by the operation of subsection (1) a person has been or will be deprived of some protection afforded by a special enactment and that corresponding protection is in all the circumstances required, or

(b) that a requirement of consent imposed by a special enactment should be saved from the operation of subsection (2), either as regards all works to which the requirement extends or as regards any description of such works, or

(c) that conditions of any descriptions should be rendered valid notwithstanding subsection (3), or

(d) that uncertainty or obscurity has resulted or is likely to result from the operation on a special enactment of the general provisions of subsection (1), (2) or (3),

he may by order make such provision as he considers appropriate for affording such protection, saving the requirement, rendering the conditions valid or modifying the special enactment, as the case may be.

(5) An order under this section shall be made by statutory instrument which shall be subject to annulment in pursuance of a resolution of either House of Parliament; and the provisions of Schedule 5 have effect with respect to the procedure for making such an order.

(6) The provisions of this section apply in relation to an instrument having effect under or by virtue of an enactment as in relation to an enactment; and references to a special enactment shall be construed accordingly.

102 Effect of this Part on other existing enactments or instruments

(1) The Secretary of State may by order make such provision amending, repealing, or preserving the effect of, any enactment passed or made before the commencement of this Part (not being a special enactment to which section 101(1), (2) or (3) applies) as appears to him appropriate in consequence of the provisions of this Part.

(2) Subject to any order under this section and (in the case of a public general Act) to any express amendment made by this Act, any such enactment which proceeds by reference to any provision of the Public Utilities Street Works Act 1950, or any other provision repealed by this Act in consequence of this Part, shall continue to have effect as if the provision referred to had not been repealed.

(3) An order under this section may, in particular, make provision in relation to—

(a) enactments providing for the keeping of records of apparatus, and

(b) enactments providing for the giving of notice of proposed street works.

(4) An order under this section may contain such transitional provisions and savings as appear to the Secretary of State to be appropriate.

(5) An order under this section shall be made by statutory instrument which shall be subject to annulment in pursuance of a resolution of either House of Parliament.

(6) Except as mentioned in section 79(6), the provisions of Schedule 5 have effect with respect to the making of an order under this section in relation to a special enactment.

(7) The provisions of this section apply in relation to an instrument having effect under or by virtue of an enactment as in relation to an enactment; and references to a special enactment shall be construed accordingly.

103 Former controlled land

(1) The following provisions apply with respect to land (not forming part of a street) in which immediately before the commencement of this Part there is apparatus placed by virtue of Schedule 1 to the Public Utilities Street Works Act 1950 (authorisation of works in certain land abutting the highway).

(2) If any person having a sufficient interest in the land gives notice to the undertaker that he objects to the continuance of the powers and rights over the land given by that Schedule, those powers and rights shall cease to have effect at the end of the period of six months from the date on which the notice was given.

For this purpose a person has a sufficient interest in the land if he is an owner, lessee or occupier of the land having an interest greater than that of tenant for a year or from year to year.

(3) The street authority shall indemnify the undertaker in respect of the costs reasonably incurred by him in or in connection with—

(a) the removal of apparatus rendered necessary by the cessation of his powers and rights under this section, and

(b) the execution of any works, or taking of any other measures, rendered necessary for the purposes of the supply or service for which the apparatus was used.

(4) Where the land becomes part of the street after the commencement of this Part, any consent which would have been required for the placing of the apparatus in the street had it been placed there immediately after the land in question became part of the street shall be deemed to have been given unconditionally.

(5) Subject to any exercise of the right conferred by subsection (2), the rights and powers of the undertaker under Schedule 1 to the Public Utilities Street Works Act 1950 continue unaffected by the repeal of that Act.

104 Meaning of "prescribed" and regulations generally

(1) In this Part "prescribed" means prescribed by the Secretary of State by regulations, which may (unless the context otherwise requires) make different provision for different cases.

(2) Regulations under this Part shall be made by statutory instrument which, unless provision to the contrary is made, shall be subject to annulment in pursuance of a resolution of either House of Parliament.

(3) Regulations under this Part may provide for references in the regulations to any specified document to operate as references to that document as revised or re-issued from time to time.

105 Minor definitions

(1) In this Part—

"apparatus" includes any structure for the lodging therein of apparatus or for gaining access to apparatus;

"carriageway" and "footway" have the same meaning as in the Highways Act 1980;

"enactment" includes an enactment contained in subordinate legislation within the meaning of the Interpretation Act 1978;

"in", in a context referring to works, apparatus or other property in a street or other place includes a reference to works, apparatus or other property under, over, across, along or upon it;

"railway" includes a light railway other than one in the nature of a tramway (see the definition of "tramway" below);

"reinstatement" includes making good;

"special enactment" means an enactment which is not a public general enactment, and includes—

(a) any Act for confirming a provisional order,
(b) any provision of a public general Act in relation to the passing of which any of the Standing Orders of the House of Lords or the House of Commons relating to Private Business applied, and
(c) any enactment to the extent that it is incorporated or applied for the purposes of a special enactment;

"statutory right" means a right (whether expressed as a right, a power or otherwise) conferred by an enactment (whenever passed or made), other than a right exercisable by virtue of a street works licence;

"traffic" includes pedestrians and animals;

"traffic authority" and "traffic sign" have the same meaning as in the Road Traffic Regulation Act 1984;

"tramway" means a system, mainly or exclusively for the carriage of passengers, using vehicles guided, or powered by energy transmitted, by rails or other fixed apparatus installed exclusively or mainly in a street.

(2) A right to execute works which extends both to a street and to other land is included in references in this Part to a right to execute works in a street in so far as it extends to the street.

(3) A right to execute works which extends to part of the street but not the whole is included in references in this Part to a right to execute works in a street; and in relation to such a right references in this Part to the street in which it is exercisable shall be construed as references to the part to which the right extends.

(4) For the purposes of this Part apparatus shall be regarded as affected by works if the effect of the works is to prevent or restrict access to the apparatus (for example, by laying other apparatus above or adjacent to it).

(5) Section 28 of the Chronically Sick and Disabled Persons Act 1970 (power to define "disability" and other expressions) applies in relation to the provisions of this Part as to the provisions of that Act.

106 Index of defined expressions

The expressions listed below are defined or otherwise fall to be construed for the purposes of this Part in accordance with the provisions indicated—

affected by (in relation to apparatus and works)	section 105(4)
apparatus	sections 89(3) and 105(1)
arbitration	section 99
bridge	section 88(1)(a)
bridge authority	section 88(1)(b)
carriageway	section 105(1)
costs	section 96
disability	(see section 105(5))
emergency works	section 52
enactment	section 105(1)
expenses	section 96
footway	section 105(1)
highway authority	section 86(1)
in (in a context referring to works, apparatus or other property in a street)	section 105(1)
licensee (in relation to a street works licence)	section 50(3)
local highway authority	section 86(1)
maintainable highway	section 86(1)
major bridge works	section 88(2)
major highway works	section 86(3)
major transport works	section 91(2)
notice	section 97

prescribed	section 104
public sewer	section 89(1)(a)
railway	section 105(1)
reinstatement	section 105(1) (and see sections 70(5) and 90(1))
relevant authority (in relation to street works)	section 49(6) (and see section 91(3))
sewer	section 89(1)(a)
sewer authority	section 89(1)(b)
special enactment	section 105(1)
statutory right	section 105(1)
street	section 48(1)
street authority	section 49(1)
street managers	section 49(4)
street works	section 48(3) (and see section 105(2) and (3))
street works licence	section 50(1)
traffic	section 105(1)
traffic authority	section 105(1)
traffic sign	section 105(1)
tramway	section 105(1)
transport authority	section 91(1)(a)
transport undertaking	section 91(1)(b)
undertaker (in relation to street works or apparatus)	sections 48(4) and(5) and 89(4)
working day	section 98(2)
works for road purposes	section 86(2).

PART IV

ROAD WORKS IN SCOTLAND

Introductory provisions

107 Roads, road works and undertakers

(1) In this Part a "road" means any way (other than a substitute road made under section 74(1) of the Roads (Scotland) Act 1984 or a waterway) whether or not there is over it a public right of passage and whether or not it is for the time being formed as a way; and the expression includes a square or court, and any part of a road.

(2) Where a road passes over a bridge or through a tunnel, references in this Part to the road include that bridge or tunnel.

(3) In this Part "road works" means works for any purposes other than roads purposes, being works of any of the following kinds executed in a road in pursuance of a statutory right or with permission granted under section 109—

(a) placing apparatus, or

(b) inspecting, maintaining, adjusting, repairing, altering or renewing apparatus, changing the position of apparatus or removing it,

or works required for or incidental to any such works (including, in particular, breaking up or opening the road, or any sewer, drain or tunnel under it, or tunnelling or boring under the road).

(4) In this Part "undertaker" in relation to road works means the person by whom the relevant statutory right is exercisable (in the capacity in which it is exercisable by him) or a person having permission under section 109 to execute road works, as the case may be.

(5) References in this Part to the undertaker in relation to apparatus in a road are to the person entitled, by virtue of a statutory right or a permission granted under section 109, to carry out in relation to the apparatus such works as are mentioned in subsection (3); and references to an undertaker having apparatus in the road, or to the undertaker to whom apparatus belongs, shall be construed accordingly.

108 The road works authority and other relevant authorities

(1) In this Part "the road works authority" in relation to a road means, subject to the following provisions—

(a) if the road is a public road, the roads authority, and

(b) if the road is not a public road, the road managers.

(2) In the case of a road for which the Secretary of State is the roads authority but in relation to which a local roads authority acts as his agent under section 4 of the Roads (Scotland) Act 1984, the local roads authority shall be regarded as the road works authority for the purposes of section 112 (the road works register) and sections 113 to 119 (advance notice and co-ordination of works).

(3) Subsection (1)(b) has effect subject to section 146 as regards the application of this Part to prospective public roads.

(4) In this Part the expression "road managers", used in relation to a road which is not a public road, means the authority, body or person liable to the public to maintain or repair the road or, if there is none, any authority, body or person having the management or control of the road.

(5) The Secretary of State may by regulations make provision for exempting road managers from provisions of this Part which would otherwise apply to them as the road works authority in relation to a road.

(6) References in this Part to the relevant authorities in relation to any road works are to the roads authority and also—

(a) where the works include the breaking up or opening in the road of a sewer vested in the local authority, that local authority;

(b) where the road is carried or crossed by a bridge vested in a transport authority, or crosses or is crossed by any other property held or used for the purposes of a transport authority, that authority; and

(c) where in any other case the road, not being a public road, is carried or crossed by a bridge, the bridge authority.

109 Permission to execute road works

(1) A road works authority may grant permission in writing, subject to such reasonable conditions as they consider appropriate, to persons to whom this section applies—

(a) to place, or to retain, apparatus in a road, and

(b) thereafter to inspect, maintain, adjust, repair, alter or renew the apparatus, change its position or remove it,

and to execute for those purposes any works required for or incidental to such works (including, in particular, breaking up or opening the road, or any sewer, drain or tunnel under it, or tunnelling or boring under the road).

(2) A person to whom permission has been granted under this section to execute works may do so without obtaining any consent which would otherwise be required to be given—

(a) by any other relevant authority in its capacity as such, or

(b) by any person in his capacity as the owner of apparatus affected by the works;

but without prejudice to the provisions of this Part as to the making of requirements by any such authority or person or as to the settlement of a plan and section and the execution of the works in accordance with them.

(3) The granting of permission under this section to a person does not dispense that person from obtaining any other consent, licence or permission which may be required; and it does not authorise the installation of apparatus for the use of which the licence of the Secretary of State is required unless and until that licence has been granted.

(4) This section applies to persons who are described in one or more of the following paragraphs—

(a) persons of a prescribed class,

(b) persons carrying out works of a prescribed class,

(c) persons carrying out works in a prescribed area.

(5) The conditions referred to in subsection (1) may include conditions as to—

(a) the payment of fees,

(b) the future cessation or withdrawal of the permission, and

(c) indemnification of the authority against claims arising out of what is permitted.

(6) Before granting permission under this section the road works authority shall give not less than 10 working days' notice to each of the following—

(a) where the works are likely to affect a sewer vested in a local authority, to that authority,

(b) where the works are to be executed in a part of a road which is carried or crossed by a bridge vested in a transport authority, or crosses or is crossed by any other property held or used for the purposes of a transport authority, to that authority,

(c) where in any other case the part of the road in which the works are to be executed is carried or crossed by a bridge, to the bridge authority,

(d) to any person who has given notice under section 113 (advance notice of certain works) of his intention to execute road works which are likely to be affected by the works to which the permission relates, and

(e) to any person having apparatus in the road which is likely to be affected by the works;

but a failure to do so does not affect the validity of the permission.

(7) Where permission has been granted under section 61 of the Roads (Scotland) Act 1984 in respect of apparatus and the road works authority consider that permission could be granted under this section in respect of that apparatus, they may cancel the permission granted under section 61 of the 1984 Act and, if they cancel that permission, they shall substitute for it permission granted in accordance with subsection (1) above.

(8) The works referred to in subsection (1) above do not include works for road purposes.

110 Prohibition of unauthorised road works

(1) It is an offence for a person other than the road works authority—

(a) to place apparatus in a road, or

(b) to break up or open a road, or a sewer, drain or tunnel under it, or to tunnel or bore under a road, for the purpose of placing, inspecting, maintaining, adjusting, repairing, altering or renewing apparatus, or of changing the position of apparatus or removing it,

otherwise than in pursuance of a statutory right or in accordance with a permission granted under section 109.

(2) A person committing an offence under this section is liable on summary conviction to a fine not exceeding level 3 on the standard scale.

(3) This section does not apply to—

(a) works for which consent or permission has been given under the Roads (Scotland) Act 1984 by a roads authority,

(b) works for road purposes, or

(c) emergency works of any description.

(4) If a person commits an offence under this section, the road works authority may—

(a) in the case of an offence under subsection (1)(a), direct him to remove the apparatus in respect of which the offence was committed, and

(b) in any case, direct him to take such steps as appear to them necessary to reinstate the road or any sewer, drain or tunnel under it.

If he fails to comply with the direction, the authority may remove the apparatus or, as the case may be, carry out the necessary works and recover from him the costs reasonably incurred by them in doing so.

111 Emergency works

(1) In this Part "emergency works" means works whose execution at the time when they are executed is required in order to put an end to, or to prevent the occurrence of, circumstances then existing or imminent (or which the person responsible for the

works believes on reasonable grounds to be existing or imminent) which are likely to cause danger to persons or property.

(2) Where works comprise items some of which fall within the preceding definition, the expression "emergency works" shall be taken to include such of the items as do not fall within that definition as cannot reasonably be severed from those that do.

(3) Where in any civil or criminal proceedings brought by virtue of any provision of this Part the question arises whether works were emergency works, it is for the person alleging that they were to prove it.

The road works register

112 The road works register

(1) A road works authority shall keep a register showing with respect to each road for which they are responsible such information as may be prescribed with respect to the road works, and such other descriptions of works as may be prescribed, executed or proposed to be executed in the road.

(2) The register shall contain such other information, and shall be kept in such form and manner, as may be prescribed.

(3) The authority shall make the register available for inspection, at all reasonable hours and free of charge—

(a) so far as it relates to restricted information, by any person having authority to execute works of any description in the road, or otherwise appearing to the authority to have a sufficient interest, and

(b) so far as it relates to information which is not restricted, by any person.

The Secretary of State may make provision by regulations as to the information which is restricted for the purposes of this subsection.

(4) The Secretary of State may make arrangements for the duties of road works authorities under this section to be discharged by means of one or more central registers kept by a person appointed in pursuance of the arrangements.

(5) If such arrangements are made the Secretary of State may require road works authorities to participate in and make contributions towards the cost of the arrangements.

(6) The Secretary of State may by regulations make provision with respect to any register kept in pursuance of this section—

(a) requiring the registration of such information as may be prescribed, and

(b) requiring the payment of such fee as may be prescribed in respect of the registration of information of any prescribed description;

and the regulations may contain provision as to the person responsible for securing the registration of the information and the person liable to pay the fee.

Notice and co-ordination of works

113 Advance notice of certain works

(1) In such cases as may be prescribed an undertaker proposing to execute road works shall give the prescribed advance notice of the works to the road works authority.

(2) Different periods of notice may be prescribed for different descriptions of works.

(3) The notice shall contain such information as may be prescribed.

(4) After giving advance notice under this section an undertaker shall comply with such requirements as may be prescribed, or imposed by the road works authority, as to the providing of information and other procedural steps to be taken for the purpose of co-ordinating the proposed works with other works of any description proposed to be executed in the road.

(5) An undertaker who fails to comply with his duties under this section commits an offence and is liable on summary conviction to a fine not exceeding level 3 on the standard scale.

114 Notice of starting date of works

(1) An undertaker proposing to begin to execute road works involving—

(a) breaking up or opening the road, or any sewer, drain or tunnel under it, or

(b) tunnelling or boring under the road,

shall give not less than 7 working days' notice (or such other notice as may be prescribed) to the road works authority, to any other relevant authority and to any other person having apparatus in the road which is likely to be affected by the works.

(2) Different periods of notice may be prescribed for different descriptions of works, and cases may be prescribed in which no notice is required.

(3) The notice shall state the date on which it is proposed to begin the works and shall contain such other information as may be prescribed.

(4) Where notice is required to be given under this section, the works shall not be begun without notice or before the end of the notice period, except with the consent of those to whom notice is required to be given.

(5) An undertaker who begins to execute any works in contravention of this section commits an offence and is liable on summary conviction to a fine not exceeding level 3 on the standard scale.

(6) In proceedings against a person for such an offence it is a defence for him to show that the contravention was attributable—

(a) to his not knowing the position, or not knowing of the existence, of another person's apparatus, or

(b) to his not knowing the identity or address of—

(i) a relevant authority, or

(ii) the person to whom any apparatus belongs,

and that his ignorance was not due to any negligence on his part or to any failure to make inquiries which he ought reasonably to have made.

(7) A notice under this section shall cease to have effect if the works to which it relates are not substantially begun before the end of the period of seven working days (or such other period as may be prescribed) beginning with the starting date specified in the notice, or such further period as may be allowed by those to whom notice is required to be given.

115 Power to give directions as to timing of works

(1) If it appears to the road works authority—

- (a) that proposed road works are likely to cause serious disruption to traffic, and
- (b) that the disruption would be avoided or reduced if the works were carried out only at certain times,

the authority may give the undertaker such directions as may be appropriate as to the times when the works may or may not be carried out.

(2) The procedure for giving a direction shall be prescribed by the Secretary of State.

(3) An undertaker who executes works in contravention of a direction under this section commits an offence and is liable on summary conviction to a fine not exceeding level 3 on the standard scale.

(4) The Secretary of State may issue or approve for the purpose of this section a code of practice giving practical guidance as to the exercise by road works authorities of the power conferred by this section; and in exercising that power a road works authority shall have regard to the code of practice.

116 Notice of emergency works

(1) Nothing in section 113 (advance notice), section 114 (notice of starting date) or section 115 (directions as to timing of works) affects the right of an undertaker to execute emergency works.

(2) An undertaker executing emergency works shall, if the works are of a kind in respect of which notice is required by section 114, give notice as soon as reasonably practicable, and in any event within two hours (or such other period as may be prescribed) of the works being begun, to the persons to whom notice would be required to be given under that section.

(3) The notice shall state his intention or, as the case may be, the fact that he has begun to execute the works and shall contain such other information as may be prescribed.

(4) An undertaker who fails to give notice in accordance with this section commits an offence and is liable on summary conviction to a fine not exceeding level 3 on the standard scale.

(5) In proceedings against a person for such an offence it is a defence for him to show that the contravention was attributable—

- (a) to his not knowing the position, or not knowing of the existence, of another person's apparatus, or
- (b) to his not knowing the identity or address of—
  - (i) a relevant authority, or
  - (ii) the person to whom any apparatus belongs,

and that his ignorance was not due to any negligence on his part or to any failure to make inquiries which he ought reasonably to have made.

117 Restriction on works following substantial works carried out for road purposes

(1) Where it is proposed to carry out substantial works in a road, the road works authority may by notice in accordance with this section restrict the execution of road works during the twelve months following the completion of those works.

For this purpose substantial works means works for road purposes, or such works together with other works, of such description as may be prescribed.

(2) The notice shall be published in the prescribed manner and shall specify the nature and location of the proposed works, the date (not being less than three months after the notice is published, or first published) on which it is proposed to begin the works, and the extent of the restriction.

(3) A copy of the notice shall be given to each of the following—

(a) where there is a sewer vested in a local authority in the part of the road to which the restriction relates, to that authority;

(b) where the part of the road to which the restriction relates is carried or crossed by a bridge vested in a transport authority, or crosses or is crossed by any other property held or used for the purposes of a transport authority, to that authority,

(c) where in any other case the part of the road to which the restriction relates is carried or crossed by a bridge, to the bridge authority,

(d) any person who has given notice under section 113 (advance notice of certain works) of his intention to execute road works in the part of the road to which the restriction relates, and

(e) any other person having apparatus in the part of the road to which the restriction relates;

but a failure to do so does not affect the validity of the restriction imposed by the notice.

(4) A notice ceases to be effective if the works to which it relates are not substantially begun—

(a) on or within one month from the date specified in the notice, or

(b) where road works are in progress in the part of the road to which the restriction relates on that date, within one month from the completion of those works.

(5) An undertaker shall not in contravention of a restriction imposed by a notice under this section break up or open the part of the road to which the restriction relates, except—

(a) to execute emergency works,

(b) with the consent of the road works authority, or

(c) in such other cases as may be prescribed.

(6) If he does—

(a) he commits an offence and is liable on summary conviction to a fine not exceeding level 3 on the standard scale, and

(b) he is liable to reimburse the road works authority any costs reasonably incurred by them in reinstating the road.

(7) The consent of the road works authority under subsection (5)(b) shall not be unreasonably withheld; and any question whether the withholding of consent is unreasonable shall be settled by arbitration.

(8) An undertaker shall be taken not to have failed to fulfil any statutory duty to afford a supply or service if, or to the extent that, his failure is attributable to a restriction imposed by a notice under this section.

118 General duty of road works authority to co-ordinate works

(1) A road works authority shall use their best endeavours to co-ordinate the execution of works of all kinds (including works for road purposes) in the roads for which they are responsible—

(a) in the interests of safety,

(b) to minimise the inconvenience to persons using the road (having regard, in particular, to the needs of people with a disability), and

(c) to protect the structure of the road and the integrity of apparatus in it.

(2) That duty extends to co-ordination with other road works authorities where works in a road for which one authority are responsible affect roads for which other authorities are responsible.

(3) The Secretary of State shall issue or approve for the purposes of this section codes of practice giving practical guidance as to the matters mentioned above; and in discharging their general duty of co-ordination a road works authority shall have regard to any such code of practice.

(4) If it appears to the Secretary of State that a road works authority are not properly discharging their general duty of co-ordination, he may direct the authority to supply him with such information as he considers necessary to enable him to decide whether that is the case and if so what action to take.

The direction shall specify the information to be provided and the period within which it is to be provided.

(5) If after the end of that period (whether or not the direction has been complied with) it appears to the Secretary of State that the authority are not properly discharging their general duty of co-ordination, he may direct the authority to take such steps as he considers appropriate for the purpose of discharging that duty.

The direction shall specify the steps to be taken and the period within which they are to be taken, and may include a requirement to make a report or periodic reports to the Secretary of State as to what steps have been taken and the results of taking them.

(6) A direction under this section may be varied or revoked by a further direction.

119 General duty of undertakers to co-operate

(1) An undertaker shall as regards the execution of road works use his best endeavours to co-operate with the road works authority and with other undertakers—

(a) in the interests of safety,

(b) to minimise the inconvenience to persons using the road (having regard, in particular, to the needs of people with a disability), and

(c) to protect the structure of the road and the integrity of apparatus in it.

(2) The Secretary of State shall issue or approve for the purposes of this section codes of practice giving practical guidance as to the matters mentioned in subsection (1); and—

(a) so far as an undertaker complies with such a code of practice he shall be taken to comply with his duty under that subsection, and

(b) a failure in any respect to comply with any such code is evidence of failure in that respect to comply with that duty.

(3) An undertaker who fails to comply with his duty under subsection (1) commits an offence and is liable on summary conviction to a fine not exceeding level 3 on the standard scale.

Roads subject to special controls

120 Protected roads

(1) The consent of the road works authority is required for the placing of apparatus by an undertaker in a protected road, except as mentioned below.

The following are "protected roads" for this purpose—

(a) any road or proposed road which is a special road in accordance with section 7 of the Roads (Scotland) Act 1984, and

(b) any road designated by the road works authority as protected.

(2) Consent is not required for the placing of apparatus—

(a) by way of renewal of existing apparatus, or

(b) in pursuance of a permission granted under section 109 of this Act (permission to execute road works) or section 61 of the Roads (Scotland) Act 1984 (permission to place and maintain apparatus under a road), except where the permission was granted before the road became a protected road.

(3) The road works authority may require the payment of—

(a) a reasonable fee in respect of the legal or other expenses incurred in connection with the giving of their consent under this section, and

(b) an annual fee of a reasonable amount for administering the consent;

and any such fee is recoverable from the undertaker.

This shall not be construed as affecting any right of the authority where they own the land on which the road is situated to grant, subject to such terms and conditions as they think fit, the right to place anything in, under or over the land.

(4) Where the apparatus is to be placed crossing the protected road and not running along it, the road works authority shall not withhold their consent unless there are special reasons for doing so.

(5) Consent to the placing of apparatus in a protected road may be given subject to conditions; and the road works authority may agree to contribute to the expenses incurred by the undertaker in complying with the conditions.

(6) Any dispute between a road works authority and an undertaker as to the withholding of consent, the imposition of conditions, or the making of contributions shall be settled by arbitration.

(7) An undertaker having a statutory duty to afford a supply or service shall not be regarded as in breach of that duty if, or to the extent that, it is not reasonably practicable to afford a supply or service by reason of anything done by the road works authority in exercise of their functions in relation to a protected road.

121 Supplementary provisions as to designation of protected roads

(1) The Secretary of State may prescribe—

(a) the criteria for designating a road as protected,

(b) the procedure for making or withdrawing such a designation, and

(c) the information to be made available by a road works authority as to the roads for the time being designated by them.

(2) Where a road has been designated as protected the road works authority may direct an undertaker to remove or change the position of apparatus placed in the road at a time when it was not so designated.

The authority shall indemnify the undertaker in respect of his reasonable expenses in complying with such a direction.

(3) Where a designation is withdrawn the road works authority may give such directions as they consider appropriate as to—

(a) the continuance in force of any conditions subject to which consent was given for the placing of apparatus in the road, and

(b) the continuance of entitlement to any contributions in respect of the expenses of an undertaker in complying with such conditions.

(4) Where a designation is made or withdrawn the road works authority may give such directions as they consider appropriate with respect to works in progress in the road when the designation comes into force or ceases to have effect.

(5) Any dispute between a road works authority and an undertaker as to the exercise by the authority of their powers under subsection (2), (3) or (4) shall be settled by arbitration.

(6) Where a road has been designated as protected, the roads authority shall indicate that it has been so designated in the list of public roads which they are obliged to maintain by virtue of section 1 or 2 of the Roads (Scotland) Act 1984.

122 Roads with special engineering difficulties

(1) The provisions of Schedule 6 have effect for requiring the settlement of a plan and section of road works to be executed in a road designated by the road works authority as having special engineering difficulties.

(2) The Secretary of State may prescribe—

(a) the criteria for designating a road as having special engineering difficulties,

(b) the procedure for making or withdrawing such a designation, and

(c) the information to be made available by a road works authority as to the roads for the time being so designated by them.

(3) Where a local roads authority are asked to designate a road as having special engineering difficulties—

(a) by a transport authority on the ground of the proximity of the road to a structure belonging to, or under the management or control of, the authority, or

(b) by an undertaker having apparatus in the road,

and decline to do so, the transport authority or undertaker may appeal to the Secretary of State who may direct that the road be designated.

(4) The designation of a road as having special engineering difficulties shall not be withdrawn except after consultation with any transport authority or undertaker at whose request the designation was made; and a designation made in pursuance of a direction by the Secretary of State shall not be withdrawn except with his consent.

(5) Where a road has been designated as having special engineering difficulties, the roads authority shall indicate that it has been so designated in the list of public roads which they are obliged to maintain by virtue of section 1 or 2 of the Roads (Scotland) Act 1984.

123 Traffic-sensitive roads

(1) Regulations made for the purposes of section 113, 114 or 116 (notices required to be given in respect of road works) may make special provision in relation to road works in a road designated by the road works authority as traffic-sensitive.

(2) The Secretary of State may prescribe—

(a) the criteria for designating a road as traffic-sensitive,

(b) the procedure for making or withdrawing such a designation, and

(c) the information to be made available by a road works authority as to the roads for the time being so designated by them.

(3) If it appears to the road works authority that the prescribed criteria are met only at certain times or on certain dates, a limited designation may be made accordingly.

In such a case the reference in subsection (1) to the execution of works in a road designated as traffic-sensitive shall be construed as a reference to works so executed at those times or on those dates.

(4) Where a road has been designated as traffic-sensitive, the roads authority shall indicate that it has been so designated in the list of public roads which they are obliged to maintain by virtue of section 1 or 2 of the Roads (Scotland) Act 1984.

General requirements as to execution of road works

124 Safety measures

(1) An undertaker executing road works shall secure—

(a) that any part of the road which is broken up or open, or is obstructed by plant or materials used or deposited in connection with the works, is adequately guarded and lit, and

(b) that such traffic signs are placed and maintained, and where necessary operated, as are reasonably required for the guidance or direction of persons using the road, and in accordance with section 120 of the Roads (Scotland) Act 1984 (duty to have regard to the needs of people with a disability).

(2) In discharging in relation to a road his duty with respect to the placing, maintenance or operation of traffic signs, an undertaker shall comply with any directions given by the traffic authority.

The power of the traffic authority to give directions under this subsection is exercisable subject to any directions given by the Secretary of State under section 65 of the Road Traffic Regulation Act 1984.

(3) The Secretary of State may issue or approve for the purposes of this section codes of practice giving practical guidance as to the matters mentioned in subsection (1); and—

(a) so far as an undertaker complies with such a code of practice he shall be taken to comply with that subsection; and

(b) a failure in any respect to comply with any such code is evidence of failure in that respect to comply with that subsection.

(4) An undertaker who fails to comply with subsection (1) or (2) commits an offence and is liable on summary conviction to a fine not exceeding level 3 on the standard scale.

(5) If it appears to the road works authority that an undertaker has failed to comply with subsection (1) or (2), they may take such steps as appear to them necessary and may recover from the undertaker the costs reasonably incurred by them in doing so.

(6) If a person without lawful authority or excuse—

(a) takes down, alters or removes any fence, barrier, traffic sign or light erected or placed in pursuance of subsection (1) or (2) above, or

(b) extinguishes a light so placed,

he commits an offence and is liable on summary conviction to a fine not exceeding level 3 on the standard scale.

125 Avoidance of unnecessary delay or obstruction

(1) An undertaker executing road works which involve—

(a) breaking up or opening the road, or any sewer, drain or tunnel under it, or

(b) tunnelling or boring under the road,

shall carry on and complete the works with all such dispatch as is reasonably practicable.

(2) An undertaker who fails to do so commits an offence and is liable on summary conviction to a fine not exceeding level 3 on the standard scale.

(3) Where an undertaker executing any road works creates an obstruction in a road to a greater extent or for a longer period than is reasonably necessary, the road works authority may by notice require him to take such reasonable steps as are specified in the notice to mitigate or discontinue the obstruction.

(4) If the undertaker fails to comply with such a notice within 24 hours of receiving it, or such longer period as the authority may specify, the authority may take the necessary steps and recover from him the costs reasonably incurred by them in doing so.

126 Qualifications of supervisors and operatives

(1) It is the duty of an undertaker executing road works involving—

(a) breaking up the road, or any sewer, drain or tunnel under it, or

(b) tunnelling or boring under the road,

to secure that, except in such cases as may be prescribed, the execution of the works is supervised by a person having a prescribed qualification as a supervisor.

(2) It is the duty of an undertaker executing road works involving—

(a) breaking up or opening the road, or any sewer, drain or tunnel under it, or

(b) tunnelling or boring under the road,

to secure that, except in such cases as may be prescribed, there is on site at all times when any such works are in progress at least one person having a prescribed qualification as a trained operative.

(3) An undertaker who fails to comply with his duty under subsection (1) or (2) commits an offence and is liable on summary conviction to a fine not exceeding level 3 on the standard scale.

(4) Regulations made by the Secretary of State for the purposes of this section may include provision with respect to—

(a) the approval of bodies conferring qualifications (and the withdrawal of such approval), and

(b) the circumstances in which a qualification may be conferred.

127 Facilities to be afforded to road works authority

(1) An undertaker executing road works shall afford the road works authority reasonable facilities for ascertaining whether he is complying with his duties under this Part.

(2) An undertaker who fails to afford the road works authority such facilities commits an offence in respect of each failure and is liable on summary conviction to a fine not exceeding level 3 on the standard scale.

128 Works likely to affect other apparatus in the road

(1) Where road works are likely to affect another person's apparatus in the road, the undertaker executing the works shall take all reasonably practicable steps—

(a) to give the person to whom the apparatus belongs reasonable facilities for monitoring the execution of the works, and

(b) to comply with any requirement made by him which is reasonably necessary for the protection of the apparatus or for securing access to it.

(2) An undertaker who fails to comply with subsection (1) commits an offence in respect of each failure and is liable on summary conviction to a fine not exceeding level 3 on the standard scale.

(3) In proceedings against a person for such an offence it is a defence for him to show that the failure was attributable—

(a) to his not knowing the position, or not knowing of the existence, of another person's apparatus, or

(b) to his not knowing the identity or address of the person to whom any apparatus belongs,

and that his ignorance was not due to any negligence on his part or to any failure to make inquiries which he ought reasonably to have made.

Reinstatement

129 Duty of undertaker to reinstate

(1) It is the duty of the undertaker by whom road works are executed to reinstate the road.

(2) He shall begin the reinstatement as soon after the completion of any part of the road works as is reasonably practicable and shall carry on and complete the reinstatement with all such dispatch as is reasonably practicable.

(3) He shall before the end of the next working day after the day on which the reinstatement is completed inform the road works authority that he has completed the reinstatement of the road, stating whether the reinstatement is permanent or interim.

(4) If it is interim, he shall complete the permanent reinstatement of the road as soon as reasonably practicable and in any event within six months (or such other period as may be prescribed) from the date on which the interim reinstatement was completed; and he shall notify the road works authority when he has done so.

(5) The permanent reinstatement of the road shall include, in particular, the reinstatement of features designed to assist people with a disability.

(6) An undertaker who fails to comply with any provision of this section commits an offence and is liable on summary conviction to a fine not exceeding level 3 on the standard scale.

(7) In proceedings against a person for an offence of failing to comply with subsection (2) it is a defence for him to show that any delay in reinstating the road was in order to avoid hindering the execution of other works, or other parts of the same works, to be undertaken immediately or shortly thereafter.

130 Materials, workmanship and standard of reinstatement

(1) An undertaker executing road works shall in reinstating the road comply with such requirements as may be prescribed as to the specification of materials to be used and the standards of workmanship to be observed.

(2) He shall also ensure that the reinstatement conforms to such performance standards as may be prescribed—

- (a) in the case of interim reinstatement, until permanent reinstatement is effected, and
- (b) in the case of permanent reinstatement, for the prescribed period after the completion of the reinstatement.

This obligation is extended in certain cases and restricted in others by the provisions of section 132 as to cases where a reinstatement is affected by subsequent works.

(3) Regulations made for the purposes of this section may make different provision in relation to different classes of excavation and different descriptions of road, and in relation to interim and permanent reinstatement.

(4) The Secretary of State may issue or approve for the purposes of this section codes of practice giving practical guidance as to the matters mentioned in subsections (1) and (2); and regulations made for the purposes of this section may provide that—

(a) so far as an undertaker complies with such a code of practice he shall be taken to comply with his duties under this section; and

(b) a failure in any respect to comply with any such code is evidence of failure in that respect to comply with those duties.

(5) An undertaker who fails to comply with his duties under this section commits an offence and is liable on summary conviction to a fine not exceeding level 3 on the standard scale.

131 Powers of road works authority in relation to reinstatement

(1) The road works authority may carry out such investigatory works as appear to them to be necessary to ascertain whether an undertaker has complied with his duties under this Part with respect to reinstatement.

If such a failure is disclosed, the undertaker shall bear the cost of the investigatory works; if not, the road works authority shall bear the cost of the investigatory works and of any necessary reinstatement.

(2) Where an undertaker has failed to comply with his duties under this Part with respect to reinstatement, he shall bear the cost of—

(a) a joint inspection with the road works authority to determine the nature of the failure and what remedial works need to be undertaken,

(b) an inspection by the authority of the remedial works in progress, and

(c) an inspection by the authority when the remedial works have been completed.

(3) The road works authority may by notice require an undertaker who has failed to comply with his duties under this Part with respect to reinstatement to carry out the necessary remedial works within such period of not less than 7 working days as may be specified in the notice.

If he fails to comply with the notice, the authority may carry out the necessary works and recover from him the costs reasonably incurred by them in doing so.

(4) If it appears to the road works authority that a failure by an undertaker to comply with his duties under this Part as to reinstatement is causing danger to users of the road, the authority may carry out the necessary works without first giving notice and may recover from him the costs reasonably incurred by them in doing so.

They shall, however, give notice to him as soon as reasonably practicable stating their reasons for taking immediate action.

132 Reinstatement affected by subsequent works

(1) The provisions of this section apply in relation to an undertaker's duty under section 130(2) to ensure that a reinstatement conforms to the prescribed performance standards for the requisite period; and references to responsibility for a reinstatement and to the period of that responsibility shall be construed accordingly.

(2) Where a reinstatement is affected by remedial works executed by the undertaker in order to comply with his duties under this Part with respect to reinstatement and the extent of the works exceeds that prescribed, the subsequent reinstatement shall be treated as a new reinstatement as regards the period of his responsibility.

(3) Where the road works authority carry out investigatory works in pursuance of section 131(1) and the investigation does not disclose any failure by the undertaker to comply with his duties under this Part with respect to reinstatement, then, to the extent that the original reinstatement has been disturbed by the investigatory works, the responsibility of the undertaker for the reinstatement shall cease.

(4) Where a reinstatement is affected by remedial works executed by the road works authority in exercise of their powers under section 131(3) or (4) (powers to act in default of undertaker)—

(a) the undertaker is responsible for the subsequent reinstatement carried out by the authority, and

(b) if the extent of the works exceeds that prescribed, the subsequent reinstatement shall be treated as a new reinstatement as regards the period of his responsibility.

(5) The following provisions apply where a reinstatement is affected by subsequent works in the road otherwise than as mentioned above.

(6) If the reinstatement is dug out to any extent in the course of the subsequent works, the responsibility of the undertaker for the reinstatement shall cease to that extent.

(7) If in any other case the reinstatement ceases to conform to the prescribed performance standards by reason of the subsequent works, the responsibility of the undertaker for the reinstatement is transferred to the person executing the subsequent works; and the provisions of this Part apply in relation to him as they would have applied in relation to the undertaker.

(8) Where there are successive subsequent works affecting a reinstatement, then as between earlier and later works—

(a) subsections (6) and (7) apply in relation to the cessation or transfer of the responsibility of the person for the time being responsible for the reinstatement; and

(b) if the reinstatement ceases to conform to the prescribed performance standards by reason of the works or any of them, it shall be presumed until the contrary is proved that this was caused by the later or last of the works.

Charges, fees and contributions payable by undertakers

133 Charge for occupation of the road where works unreasonably prolonged

(1) The Secretary of State may make provision by regulations requiring an undertaker executing road works in a public road to pay a charge to the roads authority where—

(a) the duration of the works exceeds such period as may be prescribed, and

(b) the works are not completed within a reasonable period.

(2) For this purpose "a reasonable period" means such period as is agreed by the authority and the undertaker to be reasonable or, in default of such agreement, is determined by arbitration to be reasonable, for completion of the works in question.

In default of agreement, the authority's view as to what is a reasonable period shall be acted upon pending the decision of the arbiter.

(3) The regulations may provide that if an undertaker has reason to believe that the duration of works will exceed the prescribed period he may submit to the authority an estimate of their likely duration—

(a) in the case of works in connection with the initial placing of apparatus in the road in pursuance of a permission granted under section 109 (permission to execute road works), together with his application for permission,

(b) in the case of other works (not being emergency works), together with his notice under section 114 (notice of starting date), or

(c) in the case of emergency works, as soon as reasonably practicable after the works are begun,

and that the period stated in an estimate so submitted shall be taken to be agreed by the authority to be reasonable unless they give notice, in such manner and within such period as may be prescribed, objecting to the estimate.

(4) The regulations may also provide that if it appears to the undertaker that by reason of matters not previously foreseen or reasonably foreseeable the duration of the works—

(a) is likely to exceed the prescribed period,

(b) is likely to exceed the period stated in his previous estimate, or

(c) is likely to exceed the period previously agreed or determined to be a reasonable period,

he may submit an estimate or revised estimate accordingly, and that if he does so any previous estimate, agreement or determination shall cease to have effect and the period stated in the new estimate shall be taken to be agreed by the authority to be reasonable unless they give notice, in such manner and within such period as may be prescribed, objecting to the estimate.

(5) The amount of the charge shall be determined in such manner as may be prescribed by reference to the time taken to complete the works and the extent to which the surface of the road is affected by the works.

Different rates of charge may be prescribed according to the place and time at which the works are executed and such other factors as appear to the Secretary of State to be relevant.

(6) The regulations may make provision as to the time and manner of making payment of any charge.

(7) The regulations shall provide that a roads authority may reduce the amount, or waive payment, of a charge in any particular case, in such classes of case as they may decide or as may be prescribed, or generally.

(8) The first regulations for the purposes of this section shall not be made unless a draft of them has been laid before and approved by a resolution of each House of Parliament; subsequent regulations shall be subject to annulment in pursuance of a resolution of either House of Parliament.

134 Inspection fees

(1) An undertaker executing road works shall, subject to the provisions of any scheme under this section, pay to the road works authority the prescribed fee in respect of each inspection of the works carried out by the authority.

(2) Different fees may be prescribed according to the nature or extent of the excavation or other works, the place where they are executed and such other factors as appear to the Secretary of State to be relevant.

(3) The Secretary of State may by regulations make a scheme under which undertakers pay the prescribed fee only in respect of such proportion or number of excavations or other works as may be determined in accordance with the scheme.

(4) The scheme may make provision—

(a) as to the periods and areas by reference to which the proportion or number is to be determined, and

(b) as to the intervals at which an account is to be struck between an undertaker and a road works authority and any necessary payment or repayment made;

and different provision may be made for different descriptions of undertaker and different descriptions of road works authority.

(5) Nothing in this section applies in relation to inspections in respect of which the undertaker is obliged to bear the cost under section 131(2) (inspections consequent on his failure to comply with his duties as to reinstatement).

135 Liability for cost of temporary traffic regulation

(1) Where by reason of road works—

(a) the traffic authority makes an order or issues a notice under section 14 of the Road Traffic Regulation Act 1984 (temporary prohibition or restriction of traffic), or

(b) a concessionaire issues a notice under that section by virtue of section 43(4) of this Act,

the authority or concessionaire may recover from the undertaker the whole of the costs incurred by them in connection with or in consequence of the order or notice.

(2) Those costs shall be taken to include, in particular, the cost to the authority or concessionaire—

(a) of complying with any requirement to notify the public of any matter in connection with the making, issuing or operation of the order or notice, and

(b) of providing traffic signs in connection with the prohibition or restriction of traffic by the order or notice.

136 Liability for cost of use of alternative route

(1) Where by reason of road works the use of a road is restricted or prohibited and the diverted traffic uses as an alternative route a road of a lower classification, the undertaker shall indemnify the roads authority for the latter road in respect of costs reasonably incurred by them—

(a) in strengthening the road, so far as that is done with a view to and is necessary for the purposes of its use by the diverted traffic; or

(b) in making good any damage to the road occurring in consequence of the use by it of the diverted traffic.

(2) For this purpose the order of classification of roads, from higher to lower, is as follows:

1	Trunk roads.
2	Principal roads.
3	Other classified roads.
4	Other roads.

(3) In this section, "trunk road" and "classified road" have the meanings given by section 151 of the Roads (Scotland) Act 1984 and "principal road" refers to a road classified as such by the Secretary of State under section 11 of that Act.

137 Contributions to costs of making good long-term damage

(1) The Secretary of State may make provision by regulations requiring an undertaker executing road works to contribute to the costs incurred or likely to be incurred by a road works authority in works of reconstruction or re-surfacing of the road.

(2) The regulations may provide—

(a) for a contribution to the cost of particular remedial works, or

(b) for a general contribution calculated in such manner as may be prescribed.

(3) In the former case the regulations may contain provision for apportioning the liability where the need for the remedial works is attributable to works executed by more than one person.

(4) In the latter case the regulations may provide for the amount of the contribution to vary according to the nature of the road, the description and extent of the works and such other factors as appear to the Secretary of State to be relevant.

(5) The first regulations under this section shall not be made unless a draft of them has been laid before and approved by a resolution of each House of Parliament; subsequent regulations shall be subject to annulment in pursuance of a resolution of either House of Parliament.

Duties and liabilities of undertakers with respect to apparatus

138 Records of location of apparatus

(1) An undertaker shall, except in such cases as may be prescribed, record the location of every item of apparatus belonging to him as soon as reasonably practicable after—

(a) placing it in the road or altering its position,

(b) locating it in the road in the course of executing any other works, or

(c) being informed of its location under section 139 below,

stating the nature of the apparatus and (if known) whether it is for the time being in use.

(2) The records shall be kept up to date and shall be kept in such form and manner as may be prescribed.

(3) An undertaker shall make his records available for inspection, at all reasonable hours and free of charge, by any person having authority to execute works of any description in the road or otherwise appearing to the undertaker to have a sufficient interest.

(4) If an undertaker fails to comply with his duties under this section—

(a) he commits an offence and is liable on summary conviction to a fine not exceeding level 3 on the standard scale; and

(b) he is liable to compensate any person in respect of damage or loss incurred by him in consequence of the failure.

(5) In criminal or civil proceedings arising out of any such failure it is a defence for the undertaker to show that all reasonable care was taken by him, and by his contractors and by persons in his employ or that of his contractors, to secure that no such failure occurred.

(6) An order under section 161 (power to make consequential amendments, repeals, &c.) relating to an enactment or instrument containing provision for the keeping of records of apparatus which appears to the Secretary of State to be superseded by or otherwise inconsistent with the provisions of this section—

(a) shall not be subject to the procedure provided for in Schedule 7, and

(b) may make such transitional and other provision as appears to the Secretary of State appropriate for applying in relation to records compiled under that enactment or instrument the provisions of subsections (2) to (5) above and section 139 below.

139 Duty to inform undertakers of location of apparatus

(1) A person executing works of any description in the road who finds apparatus belonging to an undertaker which is not marked, or is wrongly marked, on the records made available by the undertaker, shall take such steps as are reasonably practicable to inform the undertaker to whom the apparatus belongs of its location and (so far as appears from external inspection) its nature and whether it is in use.

(2) Where a person executing works of any description in the road finds apparatus which does not belong to him and is unable, after taking such steps as are reasonably practicable, to ascertain to whom the apparatus belongs, he shall—

(a) if he is an undertaker, note on the records kept by him under section 138(1) (in such manner as may be prescribed) the location of the apparatus he has found and its general description; and

(b) in any other case, inform the road works authority of the location and general description of the apparatus he has found.

(3) Subsections (1) and (2) have effect subject to such exceptions as may be prescribed.

(4) A person who fails to comply with subsection (1) or (2) commits an offence and is liable on summary conviction to a fine not exceeding level 3 on the standard scale.

140 Duty to maintain apparatus

(1) An undertaker having apparatus in the road shall secure that the apparatus is maintained to the reasonable satisfaction of—

(a) the road works authority, as regards the safety and convenience of persons using the road (having regard, in particular, to the needs of people with a disability), the structure of the road and the integrity of apparatus of the authority in the road, and

(b) any other relevant authority, as regards any land, structure or apparatus of theirs;

and he shall afford reasonable facilities to each such authority for ascertaining whether it is so maintained.

(2) For this purpose maintenance means the carrying out of such works as are necessary to keep the apparatus in efficient working condition (including periodic renewal where appropriate); and includes works rendered necessary by other works in the road, other than major works for road purposes, major bridge works or major transport works (as to which, see sections 143 and 144 below).

(3) If an undertaker fails to give a relevant authority the facilities required by this section—

(a) the road works authority may in such cases as may be prescribed, and

(b) any other relevant authority may in any case,

execute such works as are needed to enable them to inspect the apparatus in question, including any necessary breaking up or opening of the road.

(4) If an undertaker fails to secure that apparatus is maintained to the reasonable satisfaction of a relevant authority in accordance with this section—

(a) the road works authority may in such cases as may be prescribed, and

(b) any other relevant authority may in any case,

execute any emergency works needed in consequence of the failure.

(5) The provisions of this Part apply in relation to works executed by a relevant authority under subsection (3) or (4) as if they were executed by the undertaker; and the undertaker shall indemnify the authority in respect of the costs reasonably incurred by them in executing the works.

(6) A relevant authority who execute or propose to execute any works under subsection (3) or (4) shall give notice to any other relevant authority as soon as reasonably practicable stating the general nature of the works.

(7) Nothing in subsection (3) or (4) shall be construed as excluding any other means of securing compliance with the duties imposed by subsection (1).

141 Liability for damage or loss caused

(1) An undertaker shall compensate—

(a) the road works authority or any other relevant authority in respect of any damage or loss suffered by the authority in their capacity as such, and

(b) any other person having apparatus in the road in respect of any expense reasonably incurred in making good damage to that apparatus,

as a result of the execution by the undertaker of road works or any event of a kind mentioned in subsection (2) below.

(2) The events referred to in subsection (1) are any explosion, ignition, discharge or other event occurring to gas, electricity, water or other thing required for the purposes of a supply or service afforded by an undertaker which—

(a) at the time of or immediately before the event in question was in apparatus of the undertaker in the road, or

(b) had been in such apparatus before that event and had escaped therefrom in circumstances which contributed to its occurrence.

(3) The liability of an undertaker under this section arises—

(a) whether or not the damage or loss is attributable to negligence on his part or on the part of any person for whom he is responsible, and

(b) notwithstanding that he is acting in pursuance of a statutory duty.

(4) However, his liability under this section does not extend to damage or loss which is attributable to misconduct or negligence on the part of—

(a) the person suffering the damage or loss, or any person for whom he is responsible, or

(b) a third party, that is, a person for whom neither the undertaker nor the person suffering the damage or loss is responsible.

(5) For the purposes of this section the persons for whom a person is responsible are his contractors and any person in his employ or that of his contractors.

(6) Nothing in this section shall be taken as exonerating an undertaker from any liability to which he would otherwise be subject.

Apparatus affected by road, bridge or transport works

142 Works for road purposes likely to affect apparatus in the road

(1) This section applies to works for road purposes other than major works for road purposes (as to which see section 143 below).

(2) Where works to which this section applies are likely to affect apparatus in the road, the authority executing the works shall take all reasonably practicable steps—

(a) to give the person to whom the apparatus belongs reasonable facilities for monitoring the execution of the works, and

(b) to comply with any requirement made by him which is reasonably necessary for the protection of the apparatus or for securing access to it.

(3) An authority who fail to comply with subsection (2) commit an offence in respect of each failure and are liable on summary conviction to a fine not exceeding level 3 on the standard scale.

(4) In proceedings against an authority for such an offence it is a defence for them to show that the failure was attributable—

(a) to their not knowing the position, or not knowing of the existence, of a person's apparatus, or

(b) to their not knowing the identity or address of the person to whom any apparatus belongs,

and that their ignorance was not due to any negligence on their part or to any failure to make inquiries which they ought reasonably to have made.

143 Measures necessary where apparatus affected by major works

(1) Where an undertaker's apparatus in a road is or may be affected by major works for roads purposes, major bridge works or major transport works, the roads, bridge or transport authority concerned and the undertaker shall take such steps as are reasonably required—

(a) to identify any measures needing to be taken in relation to the apparatus in consequence of, or in order to facilitate, the execution of the authority's works,

(b) to settle a specification of the necessary measures and determine by whom they are to be taken, and

(c) to co-ordinate the taking of those measures and the execution of the authority's works,

so as to secure the efficient implementation of the necessary work and the avoidance of unnecessary delay.

(2) The Secretary of State may issue or approve for the purposes of this section a code of practice giving practical guidance as to the matters mentioned in subsection (1) and the steps to be taken by the authority and the undertaker.

(3) Any dispute between the authority and the undertaker as to any of the matters mentioned in subsection (1) shall, in default of agreement, be settled by arbitration.

(4) If the authority or the undertaker fails to comply with an agreement between them as to any of those matters, or with the decision of the arbiter under subsection (3), the authority or undertaker shall be liable to compensate the other in respect of any loss or damage resulting from the failure.

144 Sharing of cost of necessary measures

(1) Where an undertaker's apparatus in a road is affected by major works for roads purposes, major bridge works or major transport works, the allowable costs of the measures needing to be taken in relation to the apparatus in consequence of the works, or in order to facilitate their execution, shall be borne by the roads, bridge or transport authority concerned and the undertaker in such manner as may be prescribed.

(2) The regulations may make provision as to the costs allowable for this purpose.

Provision may, in particular, be made for disallowing costs of the undertaker—

(a) where the apparatus in question was placed in the road after the authority had given the undertaker the prescribed notice of their intention to execute the works, or

(b) in respect of measures taken to remedy matters for which the authority were not to blame,

and for allowing only such costs of either party as are not recoverable from a third party.

(3) Where the authority have a right to recover from a third party their costs in taking measures in relation to undertaker's apparatus but in accordance with section 143 it is determined that the measures should be taken by the undertaker, the right of the authority includes a right to recover the undertaker's costs in taking those measures and they shall account to the undertaker for any sum received.

(4) The regulations shall provide for the allowable costs to be borne by the authority and the undertaker in such proportions as may be prescribed.

Different proportions may be prescribed for different cases or classes of case.

(5) The regulations may require the undertaker to give credit for any financial benefit to him from the betterment or deferment of renewal of the apparatus resulting from the measures taken.

(6) The regulations may make provision as to the time and manner of making any payment required under this section.

Provisions with respect to particular authorities and undertakings

145 Roads authorities, roads and related matters

(1) In this Part—

"roads authority" and "local roads authority" have the same meaning as in section 151 of the Roads (Scotland) Act 1984; and

"public road" means a road which a roads authority have a duty to maintain.

(2) In this Part "works for road purposes" means—

(a) works for the maintenance of a road,

(b) works for any purpose falling within the definition of "improvement" in section 151 of that Act,

(c) the erection, maintenance, alteration or removal of traffic signs, or

(d) the construction of a crossing for vehicles across a footway or the strengthening or adaptation of a footway for use as a crossing for vehicles.

(3) In this Part "major works for roads purposes" means works of any of the following descriptions executed by the roads authority in relation to a road which consists of or includes a carriageway—

(a) reconstruction or widening of the road,

(b) substantial alteration of the level of the road,

(c) provision, alteration of the position or width, or substantial alteration in the level of a carriageway, footpath or cycle track in the road,

(d) the construction or removal of a road hump within the meaning of section 40 of the Roads (Scotland) Act 1984,

(e) works carried out in exercise of the powers conferred by section 63 of the Roads (Scotland) Act 1984 (new access over verges and footways),

(f) provision of a cattle-grid in the road or works ancillary thereto, or

(g) tunnelling or boring under the road.

146 Prospective public roads

(1) Subject to subsection (2), where a local roads authority are satisfied that a road in their area which is not a public road is likely to become a public road, they may make a declaration to that effect.

(2) Subsection (1) does not apply to a road which is under the management or control of a transport authority.

(3) The provisions of this Part apply to a road in respect of which such a declaration has been made as they apply to a public road.

(4) In relation to road works in such a road, the road works authority—

(a) shall secure the performance by undertakers of their duties under this Part, and shall exercise their powers under this Part, in such manner as is reasonably required for the protection of the road managers; and

(b) shall comply with any reasonable request as to securing performance of those duties, or as to the exercise of those powers, which may be made by the road managers.

147 Bridges, bridge authorities and related matters

(1) In this Part—

(a) references to a bridge include so much of any road as gives access to the bridge and any embankment, retaining wall or other work or substance supporting or protecting that part of the road; and

(b) "bridge authority" means the authority, body or person in whom a bridge is vested.

(2) In this Part "major bridge works" means works for the replacement, reconstruction or substantial alteration of a bridge.

(3) Where a road is carried or crossed by a bridge, any statutory right to place apparatus in the road includes the right to place apparatus in, and attach apparatus to, the structure of the bridge; and other rights to execute works in relation to the apparatus extend accordingly.

References in this Part to apparatus in the road include apparatus so placed or attached.

(4) An undertaker proposing to execute road works affecting the structure of a bridge shall consult the bridge authority before giving notice under section 114 (notice of starting date) in relation to the works.

(5) An undertaker executing such works shall take all reasonably practicable steps—

(a) to give the bridge authority reasonable facilities for monitoring the execution of the works, and

(b) to comply with any requirement made by them which is reasonably necesssary for the protection of the bridge or for securing access to it.

(6) An undertaker who fails to comply with any requirement of subsection (4) or (5) commits an offence in respect of each failure and is liable on summary conviction to a fine not exceeding level 3 on the standard scale.

(7) Subsections (4) to (6) do not apply to works in relation to which Schedule 6 applies (works in roads with special engineering difficulties).

148 Sewers

(1) An undertaker proposing to execute road works affecting a sewer vested in a local authority shall consult that authority before giving notice under section 114 (notice of starting date) in relation to the works.

(2) References in this Part to apparatus include a sewer, drain or tunnel.

(3) References to the undertaker in relation to such apparatus, or in relation to road works in connection with such apparatus, shall be construed—

(a) in the case of a sewer vested in a local authority, as references to that authority, and

(b) in any other case, as references to the authority, body or person having the management or control of the sewer, drain or tunnel.

(4) Section 128 (provisions as to works likely to affect other apparatus in the road) does not apply by virtue of subsection (2) above in relation to works likely to affect a sewer vested in a local authority if, or to the extent that, Schedule 6 (works in roads with special engineering difficulties) applies.

149 Provisions as to reinstatement of sewers, drains or tunnels

(1) The duties of an undertaker under this Part with respect to reinstatement of the road extend, in the case of road works which involve breaking up or opening a sewer, drain or tunnel under the road, to the reinstatement of the sewer, drain or tunnel.

(2) The responsible authority may by notice require an undertaker who has failed to comply with his duties under this Part with respect to reinstatement to carry out the necessary remedial works within such period of not less than 7 working days as may be specified in the notice.

If he fails to comply with the notice, the authority may carry out the necessary works and recover from him the costs reasonably incurred by them in doing so.

(3) If it appears to the responsible authority that a failure by an undertaker to comply with his duties under this Part as to reinstatement is causing danger to users of the road, the authority may carry out the necessary works without first giving notice and may recover from him the costs reasonably incurred by them in doing so.

They shall, however, give notice to him as soon as reasonably practicable stating their reasons for taking immediate action.

(4) The responsible authority for the purposes of this section is—
- (a) in the case of a sewer vested in a local authority, that authority, and
- (b) in the case of any other sewer, drain or tunnel, the authority, body or person having the management or control of it.

150 Transport authorities, transport undertakings and related matters

(1) In this Part—
- (a) "transport authority" means the authority, body or person having the control or management of a transport undertaking; and
- (b) "transport undertaking" means a railway, tramway, dock, harbour, pier, canal or inland navigation undertaking of which the activities, or some of the activities, are carried on under statutory authority.

(2) In this Part "major transport works" means substantial works required for the purposes of a transport undertaking and executed in property held or used for the purposes of the undertaking.

(3) References in this Part to a road which crosses or is crossed by property held or used for the purposes of a transport undertaking extend to cases in which the road and the property in question are at different levels.

But the transport authority shall not be treated as a relevant authority as regards undertakers' works in such a road where the property in question consists only of—
- (a) subsoil of the road which is held by the transport authority but is not used, and has not been adapted for use, for the purposes of the undertaking, or
- (b) property underground at such a depth that there is no reasonable possibility of the works affecting it.

(4) The provisions of this Part relating to a road which crosses or is crossed by property held or used for the purposes of a transport undertaking apply to a road which is or forms part of a towing-path or other way running along a canal or inland navigation,

provided the path or way is held or used, or the subsoil of it is held, for the purposes of the canal or inland navigation undertaking.

151 Special precautions as to displaying of lights

(1) An undertaker executing road works in a road which crosses, or is crossed by, or is in the vicinity of, a railway, tramway, dock, harbour, pier, canal or inland navigation, shall comply with any reasonable requirements imposed by the transport authority concerned with respect to the displaying of lights so as to avoid any risk of their—

- (a) being mistaken for any signal light or other light used for controlling, directing or securing the safety of traffic thereon, or
- (b) being a hindrance to the ready interpretation of any such signal or other light.

(2) An undertaker who fails to comply with any such requirement commits an offence and is liable on summary conviction to a fine not exceeding level 3 on the standard scale.

(3) In proceedings for such an offence it is a defence for the undertaker to show that all reasonable care was taken by him, and by his contractors and by persons in his employ or that of his contractors, to secure that no such failure occurred.

152 Works affecting level crossings or tramways

(1) This section applies to road works at a crossing of a railway on the level or which affect a tramway.

In this section "the relevant transport authority" means the authority having the management of the railway or tramway undertaking concerned.

(2) An undertaker proposing to begin to execute works to which this section applies shall give the prescribed notice to the relevant transport authority notwithstanding that such notice is not required under section 114 (notice of starting date).

The provisions of subsections (2) to (7) of that section (contents of notice, when works may be begun, &c.) apply in relation to the notice required by this subsection as in relation to a notice under subsection (1) of that section.

(3) An undertaker executing works to which this section applies shall comply with any reasonable requirements made by the relevant transport authority—

- (a) for securing the safety of persons employed in connection with the works, or
- (b) for securing that interference with traffic on the railway or tramway caused by the execution of the works is reduced so far as is practicable;

and, except where submission of a plan and section is required, he shall defer beginning the works for such further period as the relevant transport authority may reasonably request as needed for formulating their requirements under this subsection or making their traffic arrangements.

(4) Nothing in subsection (2) or (3) affects the right of an undertaker to execute emergency works.

(5) An undertaker executing emergency works shall give notice to the relevant transport authority as soon as reasonably practicable of his intention or, as the case may be, of his having begun to do so notwithstanding that such notice is not required by section 116 (notice of emergency works).

The provisions of subsections (3) and (4) of that section (contents of notice and penalty for failure to give notice) apply in relation to the notice required by this subsection as in relation to a notice under subsection (2) of that section.

Power of road works authority or district council to undertake road works

153 Power of road works authority or district council to undertake road works

(1) A road works authority or district council may enter into an agreement with an undertaker for the execution by the authority or council on behalf of the undertaker of any road works.

(2) The agreement may contain such terms as to payment and otherwise as the parties consider appropriate.

(3) Nothing in this section shall be construed as derogating from any powers exercisable by the authority or council apart from this section.

(4) This section shall cease to have effect upon such day as the Secretary of State may appoint by order made by statutory instrument which shall be subject to annulment in pursuance of a resolution of either House of Parliament.

Supplementary provisions

154 Offences

(1) Any provision of this Part imposing criminal liability in respect of any matter is without prejudice to any civil liability in respect of the same matter.

(2) Where a failure to comply with a duty imposed by this Part is continued after conviction, the person in default commits a further offence.

155 Recovery of costs or expenses

(1) Any provision of this Part enabling an authority, body or person to recover the costs or expenses of taking any action shall be taken to include the relevant administrative expenses of that authority, body or person including an appropriate sum in respect of general staff costs and overheads.

The Secretary of State may prescribe the basis on which such amounts are to be calculated; and different provision may be made for different cases or descriptions of case.

(2) Where a right to payment enuring for the benefit of a person is conferred in respect of the same matter—

(a) both under this Part and under any enactment or agreement passed or made before the commencement of this Part, or

(b) by two or more provisions of this Part,

a payment made in discharge of any of those rights shall be treated as being made in or towards satisfaction of the other or others.

(3) Where under any provision of this Part a person is entitled in certain circumstances to recover costs or expenses incurred by him in executing works or taking other steps, any dispute as to the existence of those circumstances or as to the amount recoverable shall be determined by arbitration.

This applies whether the provision is expressed as conferring a right to recover, or as imposing a liability to reimburse or indemnify or to bear the cost, but does not apply in relation to a provision expressed as providing for the charging of a fee or conferring a right to compensation or in relation to section 137 (contribution to the cost of making good long-term damage to the road).

156 Service of notices and other documents

(1) Notices required or authorised to be given for the purposes of this Part shall be given in the prescribed form.

(2) The Secretary of State may make provision by regulations as to the manner of service of notices and other documents required or authorised to be served for the purposes of this Part.

157 Reckoning of periods

(1) In reckoning for the purposes of this Part a period expressed as a period from or before a given date, that date shall be excluded.

(2) For the purposes of this Part a working day means a day other than a Saturday, Sunday, Christmas Day, Good Friday or a bank holiday; and a notice given after 4.30 p.m. on a working day shall be treated as given on the next working day.

(3) In subsection (2) a "bank holiday" means a day which is a bank holiday under the Banking and Financial Dealings Act 1971 in the locality in which the road in question is situated.

158 Arbitration

(1) Any matter which under this Part is to be settled by arbitration shall be referred for determination by a single arbiter appointed by agreement between the parties concerned or, in default of agreement, by the sheriff.

(2) In any arbitration in accordance with subsection (1) the arbiter may, and if so directed by the Court of Session shall, state a case for the decision of the Court on any question of law arising in the arbitration; and the decision of the Court shall be final unless the Court or the House of Lords give leave to appeal to the House of Lords against the decision.

(3) Leave under subsection (2) may be given on such terms as to expenses or otherwise as the Court or the House of Lords may determine.

159 Agreements inconsistent with the provisions of this Part

(1) An agreement which purports to make provision regulating the execution of road works is of no effect to the extent that it is inconsistent with the provisions of this Part.

(2) This does not affect an agreement for the waiver or variation of a right conferred on a relevant authority by any of the provisions of this Part which is made after the right has accrued and is not inconsistent with the future operation of those provisions.

160 Effect of this Part on certain existing special enactments or instruments

(1) Any special enactment passed or made before the commencement of this Part which makes or authorises the making of provision regulating the execution of road works in a manner inconsistent with the provisions of this Part shall cease to have effect; and unless a contrary intention appears no enactment passed or made after the commencement of this Part shall be construed as making or authorising the making of any such provision.

This subsection does not apply to any provision as to the obtaining of consent for the execution of the works or for any other purpose.

(2) Any special enactment passed or made before the commencement of this Part which requires the consent of a relevant authority (in its capacity as such) to the execution of road works shall cease to have effect, except as mentioned below; and unless a contrary intention appears no special enactment passed or made after the commencement of this Part shall be construed as requiring such consent.

This subsection does not apply to a consent requirement so far as it relates to—

(a) works above the surface level of the road, or

(b) works outside the limits of supply of an undertaker in relation to whom such limits are imposed.

(3) A provision made by way of condition imposed on the giving of a consent for the execution of road works is of no effect in so far as it would have been so by virtue of section 159 if it had been made by an agreement.

(4) If it appears to the Secretary of State—

(a) that by the operation of subsection (1) a person has been or will be deprived of some protection afforded by a special enactment and that corresponding protection is in all the circumstances required, or

(b) that a requirement of consent imposed by a special enactment should be saved from the operation of subsection (2), either as regards all works to which the requirement extends or as regards any description of such works, or

(c) that conditions of any descriptions should be rendered valid notwithstanding subsection (3), or

(d) that uncertainty or obscurity has resulted or is likely to result from the operation on a special enactment of the general provisions of subsection (1), (2) or (3),

he may by order make such provision as he considers appropriate for affording such protection, saving the requirement, rendering the conditions valid or modifying the special enactment, as the case may be.

(5) An order under this section shall be made by statutory instrument which shall be subject to annulment in pursuance of a resolution of either House of Parliament; and the provisions of Schedule 7 have effect with respect to the procedure for making such an order.

(6) The provisions of this section apply in relation to an instrument having effect under or by virtue of an enactment as in relation to an enactment; and references to a special enactment shall be construed accordingly.

161 Effect of this Part on other existing enactments or instruments

(1) The Secretary of State may by order make such provision amending, repealing, or preserving the effect of, any enactment passed or made before the commencement of this Part (not being a special enactment to which section 160(1), (2) or (3) applies) as appears to him appropriate in consequence of the provisions of this Part.

(2) Subject to any order under this section and (in the case of a public general Act) to any express amendment made by this Act, any such enactment which proceeds by reference to any provision of the Public Utilities Street Works Act 1950, or any other provision repealed by this Act in consequence of this Part, shall continue to have effect as if the provision referred to had not been repealed.

(3) An order under this section may, in particular, make provision in relation to—

(a) enactments providing for the keeping of records of apparatus, and

(b) enactments providing for the giving of notice of proposed road works.

(4) An order under this section may contain such transitional provisions and savings as appear to the Secretary of State to be appropriate.

(5) An order under this section shall be made by statutory instrument which shall be subject to annulment in pursuance of a resolution of either House of Parliament.

(6) Except as mentioned in section 138(6), the provisions of Schedule 7 have effect with respect to the making of an order under this section in relation to a special enactment.

(7) The provisions of this section apply in relation to an instrument having effect under or by virtue of an enactment as in relation to an enactment; and references to a special enactment shall be construed accordingly.

162 Former controlled land

(1) The following provisions apply with respect to land (not forming part of a road) in which immediately before the commencement of this Part there is apparatus placed by virtue of Schedule 1 to the Public Utilities Street Works Act 1950 (authorisation of works in certain land abutting a road).

(2) If any person having a sufficient interest in the land gives notice to the undertaker that he objects to the continuance of the powers and rights over the land given by that Schedule, those powers and rights shall cease to have effect at the end of the period of six months from the date on which the notice was given.

For this purpose a person has a sufficient interest in the land if he is an owner, lessee or occupier of the land having an interest greater than that of tenant for a year or from year to year.

(3) The road works authority shall indemnify the undertaker in respect of the costs reasonably incurred by him in or in connection with—

(a) any removal of apparatus rendered necessary by the cessation of his powers and rights under this section, and

(b) the execution of any works or taking of any other measures rendered necessary thereby for the purposes of the supply or service for which apparatus whose removal is rendered necessary was used.

(4) Where the land becomes part of the road after the commencement of this Part, any consent which would have been required for the placing of the apparatus in the road had it been placed there immediately after the land in question became part of the road shall be deemed to have been given unconditionally.

(5) Subject to any exercise of the right conferred by subsection (2), the rights and powers of the undertaker under Schedule 1 to the Public Utilities Street Works Act 1950 continue unaffected by the repeal of that Act.

163 Meaning of "prescribed" and regulations generally

(1) In this Part "prescribed" means prescribed by the Secretary of State by regulations, which may (unless the context otherwise requires) make different provision for different cases.

(2) Regulations under this Part shall be made by statutory instrument which, unless provision to the contrary is made, shall be subject to annulment in pursuance of a resolution of either House of Parliament.

(3) Regulations under this Part may provide for references in the regulations to any specified document to operate as references to that document as revised or re-issued from time to time.

164 Minor definitions

(1) In this Part—

"apparatus" includes any structure for the lodging therein of apparatus or for gaining access to apparatus;

"carriageway" and "footway" have the same meaning as in the Roads (Scotland) Act 1984;

"enactment" includes an enactment contained in subordinate legislation within the meaning of the Interpretation Act 1978.

"in", in a context referring to works, apparatus or other property in a road or other place includes a reference to works, apparatus or other property under, over, across, along or upon it;

"railway" includes a light railway other than one in the nature of a tramway (see the definition of "tramway" below);

"reinstatement" includes making good;

"special enactment" means an enactment which is not a public general enactment, and includes—

(a) any Act for confirming a provisional order,
(b) any provision of a public general Act in relation to the passing of which any of the Standing Orders of the House of Lords or the House of Commons relating to Private Business applied, and
(c) any enactment to the extent that it is incorporated or applied for the purposes of a special enactment;

"statutory right" means a right (whether expressed as a right, a power or otherwise) conferred by an enactment (whenever passed or made), other than a right exercisable by virtue of a permission granted under section 109;

"traffic" includes pedestrians and animals;

"traffic authority" and "traffic sign" have the same meaning as in the Road Traffic Regulation Act 1984;

"tramway" means a system, mainly or exclusively for the carriage of passengers, using vehicles guided, or powered by energy transmitted, by rails or other fixed apparatus installed exclusively or mainly in a road.

(2) A right to execute works which extends both to a road and to other land is included in references in this Part to a right to execute works in a road in so far as it extends to the road.

(3) A right to execute works which extends to part of the road but not the whole is included in references in this Part to a right to execute works in a road; and in relation to such a right references in this Part to the road in which it is exercisable shall be construed as references to the part to which the right extends.

(4) For the purposes of this Part apparatus shall be regarded as affected by works if the effect of the works is to prevent or restrict access to the apparatus (for example, by laying other apparatus above or adjacent to it).

(5) Section 28 of the Chronically Sick and Disabled Persons Act 1970 (power to define "disability" and other expressions) applies in relation to the provisions of this Part as to the provisions of that Act.

165 Index of defined expressions

The expressions listed below are defined or otherwise fall to be construed for the purposes of this Part in accordance with the provisions indicated—

affected by (in relation to apparatus and works)	section 164(4)
apparatus	section 148(2) and 164
arbitration	section 158
bridge	section 147(1)(a)
bridge authority	section 147(1)(b)
carriageway	section 164
costs	section 155
disability	(see section 164(4))
emergency works	section 111
enactment	section 164
expenses	section 155
footway	section 164
in (in a context referring to works, apparatus or other property in a road)	section 164

local roads authority	section 145(1)
major bridge works	section 147(2)
major works for roads purposes	section 145(3)
major transport works	section 150(2)
notice	section 156
prescribed	section 163
public road	section 145(1)
railway	section 164
reinstatement	section 164 (and see sections 129(5) and 149(1))
relevant authority (in relation to road works)	section 108(6) (and see section 150(3))
road	section 107(1)
road managers	section 108(4)
road works	section 107(3) (and see section 164(2) and (3))
road works authority	section 108(1)
roads authority	section 145(1)
special enactment	section 164(1)
statutory right	section 164(1)
traffic	section 164(1)
traffic authority	section 164(1)
traffic sign	section 164(1)
tramway	section 164(1)
transport authority	section 150(1)(a)
transport undertaking	section 150(1)(b)
undertaker (in relation to road works or apparatus)	sections 107(4) and (5) and 148(3)
working day	section 157(2)
works for road purposes	section 145(2).

PART V

GENERAL

166 Offences by bodies corporate or Scottish partnerships

(1) Where an offence under this Act committed by a body corporate is proved to have been committed with the consent or connivance of, or to be attributable to any neglect

on the part of, a director, manager, secretary or other similar officer of the body, or a person purporting to act in any such capacity, he as well as the body corporate is guilty of the offence and liable to be proceeded against and punished accordingly.

In relation to a body corporate whose affairs are managed by its members "director" means a member of the body corporate.

(2) Where an offence under this Act is committed in Scotland by a Scottish partnership and is proved to have been committed with the consent or connivance of, or to be attributable to any neglect on the part of, a partner, he as well as the partnership is guilty of the offence and liable to be proceeded against and punished accordingly.

167 Crown application

(1) The provisions of section 327 of the Highways Act 1980 (application of Act to Crown land) apply in relation to the provisions of Part I of this Act (new roads in England and Wales) as in relation to the provisions of that Act; and the provisions of section 146 of the Roads (Scotland) Act 1984 (application of Act to Crown land) apply in relation to the provisions of Part II of this Act (new roads in Scotland) as in relation to the provisions of that Act.

(2) Subject to any regulations under subsection (3), the provisions of Parts I and II of this Act have effect in relation to persons in the public service of the Crown, vehicles belonging to, or used for the purposes of, a Minister of the Crown or Government department and things done, or omitted to be done, in connection with such vehicles by such persons as they have effect in relation to other persons or vehicles.

(3) The Secretary of State may by regulations provide that in their application in relation to—

(a) vehicles belonging to the Crown and used for naval, military or air force purposes,

(b) vehicles used for the purposes of any such body, contingent or detachment of the forces of any country as is a visiting force for the purposes of any of the provisions of the Visiting Forces Act 1952, or

(c) vehicles used for the purposes of any headquarters or organisation designated by an Order in Council under section 1 of the International Headquarters and Defence Organisations Act 1964,

the provisions of Parts I and II of this Act shall have effect subject to such modifications as may be prescribed.

For this purpose "modifications" includes additions, omissions and alterations.

(4) The provisions of Parts III and IV of this Act (street works in England and Wales and road works in Scotland) bind the Crown.

(5) Nothing in subsection (4) shall be construed as authorising the bringing of proceedings for a criminal offence against a person acting on behalf of the Crown.

(6) Regulations under this section shall be made by statutory instrument which shall be subject to annulment in pursuance of a resolution of either House of Parliament.

168 Minor and consequential amendments and repeals

(1) The enactments specified in Schedule 8 have effect with the amendments specified there which are minor amendments and amendments consequential on the provisions of this Act.

In that Schedule—

Part I contains amendments of the Highways Act 1980,

Part II contains amendments of the Road Traffic Regulation Act 1984,

Part III contains amendments of the Roads (Scotland) Act 1984, and

Part IV contains amendments of other enactments.

(2) The enactments mentioned in Schedule 9 are repealed to the extent specified there.

169 Extent

(1) The following provisions of this Act extend to England and Wales—

Part I (new roads in England and Wales),

Part III (street works in England and Wales),

the provisions of Schedule 8 (minor and consequential amendments) and Schedule 9 (repeals) so far as relating to enactments which extend to England and Wales, and

the other provisions of this Part so far as relating to the above provisions.

(2) The following provisions of this Act extend to Scotland—

Part II (new roads in Scotland),

Part IV (road works in Scotland),

the provisions of Schedule 8 (minor and consequential amendments) and Schedule 9 (repeals) so far as relating to enactments which extend to Scotland, and

the other provisions of this Part so far as relating to the above provisions.

(3) The following provisions of this Act extend to Northern Ireland—

the provisions of Schedule 8 (minor and consequential amendments) and Schedule 9 (repeals) so far as relating to enactments which extend to Northern Ireland, and

the other provisions of this Part so far as relating to the above provisions.

170 Commencement

(1) The provisions of this Act come into force on such day as the Secretary of State may appoint by order made by statutory instrument; and different days may be appointed for different provisions and different purposes.

(2) An order bringing into force any provision may contain such transitional provisions and savings as appear to the Secretary of State to be necessary or expedient.

171 Short title

This Act may be cited as the New Roads and Street Works Act 1991.

SCHEDULES

SCHEDULE 1

Section 5(2).

SUPPLEMENTARY PROVISIONS AS TO TERMINATION OF CONCESSION

Introductory

1 The provisions of this Schedule apply in relation to the transfer of property, rights and liabilities to the highway authority on the termination of a concession agreement (referred to below as "the ending of the concession").

Property to vest free from security rights

2 (1) Property vesting in the highway authority shall do so free from any mortgage, charge, lien or other security to which it was subject immediately before the ending of the concession.

(2) This does not affect the liability secured.

Recovery of property taken in distress, &c.

3 (1) Where before the ending of the concession possession of any property vesting in the highway authority has been taken in pursuance of any legal process or distress, the highway authority may recover it from any person in possession of it without being required to discharge the liability in respect of which the process or distress was issued or levied.

(2) This does not affect the liability in respect of which the process or distress was issued or levied.

Validity of previous discharge of liabilities

4 Where a liability has been discharged before the ending of the concession which if it had subsisted immediately before the ending of the concession would have fallen to be transferred to the highway authority, nothing in the Insolvency Act 1986—

(a) affects the validity of anything done by the concessionaire or any other person in discharging the liability,

(b) authorises a court to make an order affecting the property of, or imposing an obligation on, any person in consequence of or in connection with the receipt by him or by any other person of a payment made, property transferred or other benefit provided by the concessionaire or any other person in discharging that liability, or

(c) shall be treated as giving rise to a trust affecting money or property so transferred.

Property subject to covenants, conditions or restrictions

5 Except as provided by paragraph 2, property vesting in the highway authority shall be held by the authority subject to all covenants, conditions and restrictions subject to which the property was held by the concessionaire.

Transfer of agreements, &c.

6 (1) Subject to the concession agreement and to paragraph 2, all agreements and other transactions entered into or effected by the concessionaire and subsisting immediately before the ending of the concession, in so far as they relate to property, rights or liabilities transferred to the highway authority shall have effect with the substitution of the authority for the concessionaire.

(2) Accordingly—

(a) such an agreement or transaction may be enforced by or against the highway authority, and

(b) references to the concessionaire in an agreement (whether or not in writing) and in a deed, bond or other instrument or document, so far as relating to the property, rights or liabilities mentioned above shall be taken after the ending of the concession as referring to the highway authority.

Legal or other proceedings

7 (1) Subject to the concession agreement, all legal or other proceedings begun before the ending of the concession and relating to property, rights or liabilities transferred to the highway authority, other than proceedings for enforcing a security from which the property is released by virtue of paragraph 2, may be carried on with the substitution of the highway authority for the concessionaire.

(2) Such proceedings may be amended in such manner as may be necessary for that purpose.

Transfer of employees

8 For the purposes of the Transfer of Undertakings (Protection of Employment) Regulations 1981, or any regulations replacing those regulations, the concessionaire shall be treated as transferring to the highway authority an undertaking which, if a new concessionaire is appointed, the authority shall be treated as then transferring to the new concessionaire.

SCHEDULE 2

Section 6(3).

PROCEDURE IN CONNECTION WITH TOLL ORDERS

Publicity for proposals

1 (1) Where the Secretary of State proposes to make a toll order, he shall prepare a draft of the order and shall publish in at least one local newspaper circulating in the area in which the proposed special road is to be situated, and in the London Gazette, a notice—

(a) stating the general effect of the proposed order;

(b) naming a place in that area where a copy of the draft order may be inspected by any person free of charge at all reasonable hours during a period specified in the notice, being a period of not less than six weeks from the date of the publication of the notice; and

(c) stating that, within that period, any person may by notice to the Secretary of State object to the making of the order.

(2) Where a toll order is submitted to the Secretary of State by a local highway authority, the authority shall publish in at least one local newspaper circulating in the area in which the proposed special road is to be situated, and in the London Gazette, a notice—

(a) stating the general effect of the order as submitted to the Secretary of State;

(b) naming a place in that area where a copy of the order may be inspected by any person free of charge at all reasonable hours during a period specified in the notice, being a period of not less than six weeks from the date of the publication of the notice; and

(c) stating that, within that period, any person may by notice to the Secretary of State object to the confirmation of the order.

(3) Where the special road to which the toll order relates is to be subject to a concession, the Secretary of State or the local highway authority shall make available for inspection with the copy of the draft order or of the order, as the case may be, a statement containing such information as may be prescribed with respect to the concessionaire and the concession agreement.

The notice under sub-paragraph (1) or (2) shall indicate that such a statement will be so available for inspection.

(4) In sub-paragraph (3) "prescribed" means prescribed by the Secretary of State by regulations made by statutory instrument which shall be subject to annulment in pursuance of a resolution of either House of Parliament.

2 (1) The Secretary of State or the local highway authority, as the case may be, shall serve on every local authority in whose area any part of the route of the proposed special road is situated a copy of the notice published under paragraph 1(1) or (2) and of the draft order or of the order, as the case may be.

(2) The copies must be served not later than the day on which the notice is published or, if it is published on two or more days, the day on which it is first published.

(3) In sub-paragraph (1) "local authority" means a county, district or London borough council or the Common Council of the City of London.

3 If it appears to the Secretary of State or, as the case may be, the local highway authority to be desirable to do so, he or they shall take such steps, in addition to those required by paragraphs 1 and 2, as will in his or their opinion secure that additional publicity is given in the area affected by the relevant special road scheme to the proposals contained in the order.

4 (1) Before or after the end of the period specified in the notice in pursuance of paragraph 1(1) or (2), the Secretary of State or the local highway authority, as the case may be, may by a further notice published in the same manner substitute a longer period for that specified in the first notice.

(2) Paragraph 2 applies with respect to service of a copy of any such further notice as in relation to the first notice.

Making of objections

5 (1) A person who objects to the making or confirmation of a toll order shall include in the notice of objection a statement of the grounds of objection.

(2) If that is not done, the Secretary of State may disregard the objection.

Local inquiry

6 (1) If an objection is received by the Secretary of State within the period specified for making objections, and is not withdrawn, then—

- (a) if the objection is from a local authority on whom a copy of the notice is required to be served under paragraph 2, the Secretary of State shall cause a local inquiry to be held;
- (b) if the objection is from any other person appearing to the Secretary of State to be affected, he shall cause a local inquiry to be held unless he is satisfied that in the circumstances of the case it is unnecessary.

(2) The period specified for making objections means the period specified in the notice under paragraph 1(1) or (2) or any longer period substituted by a further notice under paragraph 1(3).

Making or confirmation of order

7 (1) The Secretary of State, after considering—

- (a) any objections which are not withdrawn, and
- (b) where a local inquiry is held, the report of the person who held the inquiry,

may make or confirm the order either without modification or subject to such modifications as he thinks fit.

(2) Where he proposes to make or confirm the order subject to modifications which will in his opinion make a substantial change in the order, he shall—

- (a) notify any person who appears to him to be likely to be affected by the proposed modifications,
- (b) give that person an opportunity of making representations with respect to the modifications within such reasonable period as he may specify, and
- (c) consider any representations made to him within that period with respect to the proposed modifications.

Notice of making or confirmation of order

8 As soon as may be after a toll order has been made or confirmed by the Secretary of State, he shall publish in the London Gazette, and in such other manner as he thinks best adapted for informing persons affected, a notice stating that the order has been made or confirmed and naming a place where a copy of it may be inspected free of charge at all reasonable hours.

Special parliamentary procedure where existing highway appropriated or transferred

9 (1) A toll order shall be subject to special parliamentary procedure where—

(a) the relevant special road scheme provides for the appropriation by or transfer to the special road authority of an existing highway comprised in the route prescribed by the scheme, and

(b) the toll order authorises the charging of tolls for the use of that existing highway or any part of it,

unless the Secretary of State is satisfied as regards all classes of traffic entitled to use the existing highway that another reasonably convenient route free of toll is available, or will be provided before the date on which the appropriation or transfer takes effect, and certifies accordingly.

(2) Where the Secretary of State proposes to give such a certificate, he shall—

(a) give public notice of his intention to do so,

(b) afford an opportunity to all persons interested to make representations and objections, and

(c) cause a public local inquiry to be held if it appears to him to be expedient to do so, having regard to representations or objections made,

and before deciding whether to give the certificate he shall consider any representations and objections made and, if an inquiry has been held, the report of the person who held the inquiry.

(3) As soon as may be after giving a certificate, the Secretary of State shall publish in the London Gazette, and in such other manner as he thinks best for informing persons affected, a notice stating that the certificate has been given.

Challenge to validity of order or certificate

10 (1) If a person aggrieved by a toll order desires to question the validity of it, or of any provision contained in it, on the ground—

(a) that it is not within the powers of this Act, or

(b) that any requirement of this Act has not been complied with,

he may within six weeks after the publication (or first publication) of the notice required by paragraph 8 make an application for the purpose to the High Court.

(2) The court may on such an application by interim order suspend the operation of the toll order, or any provision of it, either generally or so far as the interests of the applicant are affected, until the final determination of the proceedings.

(3) If on an application under this paragraph the court is satisfied—

(a) that the order, or any provision of it, is not within the powers of this Act, or

(b) that the interests of the applicant have been substantially prejudiced by a failure to comply with any such requirement as aforesaid,

the court may quash the order or any provision of it.

(4) If the court quashes the order, the relevant special road scheme shall also cease to have effect.

(5) Except as provided by this paragraph, the order shall not be questioned in any legal proceedings whatsoever, either before or after it is made or confirmed, and shall become operative on such date as is specified in the order.

11 (1) In relation to a toll order which is subject to special parliamentary procedure—

(a) if the order is confirmed by Act of Parliament under section 6 of the Statutory Orders (Special Procedure) Act 1945, paragraph 10 above does not apply;

(b) in any other case, that paragraph has effect subject to the following modifications—

(i) the reference in sub-paragraph (1) to the date on which the notice required by paragraph 8 is published (or first published) shall be construed as a reference to the date on which the order becomes operative under the Act of 1945, and

(ii) in sub-paragraph (5) the words "and shall become operative" to the end shall be omitted.

(2) The provisions of paragraph 10(1) to (3) and (5) above apply in relation to a certificate under paragraph 9 as in relation to a toll order, subject to the following modifications—

(a) the reference in sub-paragraph (1) to the notice required by paragraph 8 shall be construed as a reference to the notice required by paragraph 9(3), and

(b) in sub-paragraph (5) for "made or confirmed" substitute "given" and omit the words from "and shall become operative" to the end.

SCHEDULE 3

Section 50(4).

STREET WORKS LICENCES

Grant of licence

1 Before granting a street works licence the street authority shall give not less than 10 working days' notice to each of the following—

(a) where the works are likely to affect a public sewer, to the sewer authority,

(b) where the works are to be executed in a part of a street which is carried or crossed by a bridge vested in a transport authority, or crosses or is crossed by any other property held or used for the purposes of a transport authority, to that authority,

(c) where in any other case the part of the street in which the works are to be executed is carried or crossed by a bridge, to the bridge authority,

(d) to any person who has given notice under section 54 (advance notice of certain works) of his intention to execute street works which are likely to be affected by the works to which the licence relates, and

(e) to any other person having apparatus in the street which is likely to be affected by the works;

but a failure to do so does not affect the validity of the licence.

2 The street authority may require the payment of—

(a) a reasonable fee in respect of legal or other expenses incurred in connection with the grant of a street works licence, and

(b) an annual fee of a reasonable amount for administering the licence;

and any such fee is recoverable from the licensee.

This shall not be construed as affecting any right of the authority where they own the land on which the street is situated to grant for such consideration as they think fit the right to place anything in, under or over the land.

Conditions attached to licence

3 A street authority may attach to a street works licence such conditions as they consider appropriate—

(a) in the interests of safety,

(b) to minimise the inconvenience to persons using the street (having regard, in particular, to the needs of people with a disability), or

(c) to protect the structure of the street and the integrity of apparatus in it.

4 Where assignment of a street works licence is permitted, a condition may be attached requiring the consent of the street authority to any assignment.

Notice of change of ownership, &c.

5 (1) Where the licensee under a street works licence proposes—

(a) to cease using or abandon the apparatus, or

(b) to part with his interest in the apparatus,

he shall give the street authority at least six weeks' notice before doing so.

(2) Where the licensee under a street works licence granted to the owner of land and his successors in title proposes to part with his interest in the land, he shall before doing so give notice to the street authority stating to whom the benefit of the licence is to be transferred.

(3) A person who fails to comply with an obligation under this paragraph commits an offence and is liable on summary conviction to a fine not exceeding level 3 on the standard scale.

Withdrawal of licence

6 (1) The street authority may by notice in writing served on the licensee withdraw a street works licence—

(a) if the licensee fails to comply with any provision of this Part or any condition of the licence,

(b) if the authority become aware that the licensee—

(i) has ceased to use or has abandoned the apparatus, or intends to do so, or

(ii) has parted with or intends to part with his interest in the apparatus in a case where assignment of the licence is prohibited, or

(c) if the authority consider the withdrawal of the licence is necessary for the purpose of the exercise of their functions as street authority.

(2) The withdrawal takes effect at the end of such period beginning with the date of service as may be specified in the notice.

The period shall not be less than 7 working days in the case of a withdrawal under sub-paragraph (1)(a) or (b), and shall not be less than three months in the case of a withdrawal under sub-paragraph (1)(c).

Removal of apparatus

7 (1) Where a street works licence expires or is withdrawn or surrendered, the street authority may remove the apparatus to which the licence relates or alter it in such manner as they think fit and reinstate the street, and may recover from the former licensee the expenses incurred by them in doing so.

(2) If they are satisfied that the former licensee can, within such reasonable time as they may specify, remove the apparatus or alter it in such manner as they may require and reinstate the street, they may authorise him to do so at his own expense.

(3) Before executing any works under this paragraph the street authority or the former licensee, as the case may be, shall give not less than 7 working days' notice to any person whose apparatus is likely to be affected and shall satisfy their requirements as to the method of executing the works and as to the supervision of the works by them.

(4) In this paragraph and paragraph 8 below "the former licensee" means the person who immediately before the expiry, withdrawal or surrender of a street works licence was the licensee or, if that person has died, his personal representatives.

Obligation of licensee to indemnify street authority

8 (1) The licensee under a street works licence shall indemnify the street authority against any claim in respect of injury, damage or loss arising out of—

(a) the placing or presence in the street of apparatus to which the licence relates, or

(b) the execution by any person of any works authorised by the licence;

and the former licensee shall indemnify the street authority against any claim in respect of injury, damage or loss arising out of the execution by the authority or the licensee of any works under paragraph 7.

(2) The liability of a licensee or former licensee under this paragraph arises—

(a) whether or not the damage or loss is attributable to negligence on their part or on the part of any person for whom they are responsible, and

(b) notwithstanding that they are acting in pursuance of a statutory duty.

(3) However, their liability does not extend to damage or loss which is attributable to misconduct or negligence on the part of—

(a) the street authority or a person for whom the authority are responsible, or

(b) a third party, that is, a person for whom neither the licensee or former licensee nor the authority are responsible.

(4) For the purposes of this paragraph the persons for whom a person is responsible are his contractors and any person in his employ or that of his contractors.

Appeal against decision of local highway authority

9 (1) Where the apparatus in respect of which an application for a street works licence is made to a local highway authority is to be placed or retained on a line crossing the street, and not along the line of the street, a person aggrieved by—

(a) the refusal of the authority to grant him a licence,

(b) their refusal to grant a licence except on terms prohibiting its assignment, or

(c) any terms or conditions of the licence granted to him,

may appeal to the Secretary of State.

(2) The procedure on an appeal shall be such as may be prescribed.

(3) Where on an appeal the Secretary of State reverses or varies the decision of the local highway authority, it is the duty of that authority to give effect to his decision.

SCHEDULE 4

Section 63(1).

STREETS WITH SPECIAL ENGINEERING DIFFICULTIES

Introductory

1 In this Schedule a "street with special engineering difficulties" means a street for the time being designated under section 63 as having special engineering difficulties.

Requirement of plan and section

2 (1) In a street with special engineering difficulties street works (other than emergency works) involving—

(a) breaking up or opening the street, or any sewer, drain or tunnel under it, or

(b) tunnelling or boring under the street,

shall not be executed until a plan and section of the works have been settled by agreement between the undertaker and each of the relevant authorities or by arbitration.

(2) For that purpose an undertaker proposing to execute any such works shall submit a plan and section of them to each relevant authority.

3 Emergency works may be executed without a plan and section being so submitted or settled, but as soon as is reasonably practicable after the execution of the works the undertaker shall furnish a plan and section of the works to each relevant authority.

4 (1) In the case of a street which is not a maintainable highway and which the street managers have no liability to the public to maintain or repair, the undertaker may give the street managers a notice stating—

(a) the general effect of the works proposed or, as the case may be, of the emergency works executed, and

(b) that it is a notice given for the purposes of this paragraph.

(2) Where such a notice is given paragraphs 2 and 3 do not apply if the street managers do not, within 10 working days from the date on which the notice was given to them, give notice to the undertaker requiring the submission or furnishing of a plan and section to them.

5 (1) A relevant authority to whom a plan and section of works are required to be submitted or furnished may accept as, or in lieu of, a plan and section any description of the works, whether in diagram form or not, which appears to them to be sufficient.

(2) References in this Schedule to a plan and section include any such description so submitted or furnished to the form of which the relevant authority have not objected within the time allowed under paragraph 7(2) below.

6 If an undertaker—

(a) executes any works in contravention of paragraph 2, or

(b) fails to furnish a plan and section in accordance with paragraph 3,

he commits an offence and is liable on summary conviction to a fine not exceeding level 3 on the standard scale.

Procedure on submission of plan and section

7 (1) A relevant authority to whom there is submitted a plan and section of street works proposed to be executed in a street with special engineering difficulties shall give notice to the undertaker—

(a) approving the plan and section without modification, or

(b) objecting to them in form as being on too small a scale or giving insufficient particulars, or

(c) approving them subject to modifications specified in the notice, or

(d) disapproving them.

(2) The notice shall be given without avoidable delay, and at the latest before the end of the period of—

(a) 7 working days in the case of a plan and section of works relating only to—

(i) a service pipe or service line, or

(ii) overhead electric lines or telecommunication apparatus, and

(b) one month in any other case;

and as between the undertaker and a relevant authority who do not duly give notice before the end of that period, the plan and section as submitted shall be deemed to have been settled by agreement.

(3) The reference in sub-paragraph (2)(a)(i) to a service pipe or service line is to—

(a) a pipe or line through or by means of which a supply of gas, electricity or water is afforded or intended to be afforded to premises—

(i) directly from premises from which the supply originates, or

(ii) from a main, that is, a pipe or line for affording a general supply;

(b) a pipe through or by means of which sewerage services are afforded, or intended to be afforded, which is a private sewer or drain within the meaning of the Water Act 1989; or

(c) underground telecommunication apparatus for the purpose of providing a service by means of a telecommunication system to or from particular premises (as opposed to apparatus for the general purposes of such a system).

But so much of any such pipe, line or apparatus as is placed, or intended to be placed, for a continuous length of 100 metres or more in a maintainable highway shall be treated as not being a service pipe or service line.

(4) In this paragraph—

"electric line" has the same meaning as in Part I of the Electricity Act 1989;

"telecommunication apparatus" has the same meaning as in Schedule 2 to the Telecommunications Act 1984; and

"telecommunication system" has the meaning given by section 4(1) of that Act (read with subsection (2) of that section).

8 (1) Where a relevant authority give notice approving the plan and section subject to modifications, or disapproving the plan and section, they shall state their reasons for doing so.

(2) If a relevant authority duly give notice—

(a) objecting to the plan and section in form, or

(b) approving them subject to modifications to which the undertaker does not agree, or

(c) disapproving them,

then, unless the notice is withdrawn, the undertaker may refer the matter to arbitration.

(3) If the notice is withdrawn, the plan and section as submitted shall be deemed to have been settled by agreement between the relevant authority and the undertaker.

9 A sewer authority or bridge authority may not give notice—

(a) approving a plan and section subject to modifications, or

(b) disapproving a plan and section,

on grounds other than such as relate to the injurious effect of the proposed works on their sewer or, as the case may be, on the structure or stability of their bridge.

Settlement of plan and section by arbitration

10 (1) The duty of the arbitrator where a matter is referred to arbitration is to settle a plan and section of works of the kind proposed, as works to be executed in the street.

(2) He may require the undertaker to submit to him a plan and section in such form, require the relevant authority to submit to him such observations on a plan and section submitted to him, and require the undertaker or the relevant authority to furnish him with such information and to take such other steps, as appear to him to be requisite.

(3) He may treat compliance with any such requirement made of the undertaker as a condition of his proceeding with the settlement of a plan and section, and compliance with any such requirement made of the relevant authority as a condition of his settling a plan and section otherwise than as proposed by the undertaker.

11 (1) Where the reference relates to the placing, altering or changing the position of apparatus in a street which is carried or crossed by a bridge, then, if the arbitrator is satisfied—

(a) that the execution of the works would be likely to affect injuriously the structure or stability of the bridge, and

(b) that it is not practicable to meet objection on that ground to the plan and section submitted,

he shall so declare, and shall not settle any plan and section of those works on the reference.

(2) This does not affect the right of the undertaker to submit another plan and section.

Objection to works executed without plan and section being settled

12 (1) This paragraph applies where street works have been executed in a street with special engineering difficulties without a plan and section having been settled with the street authority or another relevant authority, whether the works were executed in contravention of paragraph 2 above or were emergency works.

(2) The authority in question may, by notice to the undertaker, object to any of the works; and after affording the undertaker an opportunity to enter into an agreement with them for meeting the objection, may refer the matter to arbitration.

(3) The arbitrator may direct the alteration of the works to conform to a plan and section settled by him, or the removal of any apparatus placed in the execution of the works, and the undertaker shall comply with any such direction.

(4) In settling the terms of any such direction the arbitrator shall satisfy himself that compliance with it will not involve any undue interruption or restriction of the supply or service for the purposes of which the works were executed.

(5) If an undertaker fails to execute works in accordance with a direction under this paragraph, he commits an offence and is liable on summary conviction to a fine not exceeding level 3 on the standard scale.

Execution of works in accordance with plan and section

13 (1) An undertaker executing street works in a street with special engineering difficulties shall, where a plan and section have been settled, execute the works in accordance with the plan and section as settled or, if each of the relevant authorities agrees to the modification of the plan or section, in accordance with them as so modified.

(2) If an undertaker fails to comply with sub-paragraph (1) he commits an offence and is liable on summary conviction to a fine not exceeding level 3 on the standard scale.

SCHEDULE 5

Sections 101(4) and 102(6).

PROCEDURE FOR MAKING CERTAIN ORDERS UNDER PART III

Publication of proposals

1 Where the Secretary of State proposes to make an order under section 101 (effect of Part III on certain existing special enactments or instruments), or an order under section 102 (effect of Part III on other existing enactments or instruments) relating to a special enactment or instrument, he shall publish in the London Gazette, and in at least one newspaper circulating in the area in relation to which the enactment or instrument in question has effect, a notice—

(a) stating the general effect of the proposed order,

(b) specifying a place in that area where a copy of the draft order may be inspected by any person free of charge at all reasonable hours or may be purchased by any person at a reasonable charge, and

(c) stating that any person may, by notice given to the Secretary of State within three months from the date of the publication of the notice, object to the proposed order.

Notice to parties affected

2 Not later than the day on which the notice is published or, if it is published on two or more days, the day on which it is first published, the Secretary of State shall

furnish each of the parties specified below by reference to the nature of the order with a copy of the draft order.

Order under section 101(4)(a) relating to protection afforded by an enactment or instrument	The undertaker by whom the power is exercisable and each of the persons to whom the protection in question was afforded.
Order under section 101(4)(b) relating to requirement of consent	The person whose consent would be required and the undertaker who would be required to obtain the consent.
Order under section 101(4)(c) rendering condition valid	The person by whom the condition would be imposed and the undertaker who would be required to comply with it.
Order under section 101(4)(d) modifying enactment or instrument to remove uncertainty or obscurity	As indicated above, according to whether the order relates to the protection afforded by an enactment or instrument, a consent requirement or the validity of a condition.
Order under section 102 amending, repealing or preserving effect of enactment or instrument	Any person whose interests are specially affected by the proposed provision.

Local inquiry

3 (1) The Secretary of State shall cause a local inquiry to be held if an objection to the proposed order is received by him—

(a) from a person required to be furnished with a copy of the draft order within three months from the date of his being furnished therewith, or

(b) from any other person appearing to him to be affected within three months from the day on which the notice of the proposed order is published, or if it is published on two or more days from the later or latest of them,

and the objection is not withdrawn.

(2) In the case of an objection made otherwise than by a person required to be furnished with a copy of the draft order, the Secretary of State may dispense with such an inquiry if he is satisfied that it is unnecessary.

4 (1) The provisions of section 250(2) to (5) of the Local Government Act 1972 (which relate to the giving of evidence at, and the defraying of costs of, inquiries) apply in relation to a local inquiry held under paragraph 3.

(2) Subsection (4) of that section (which requires the costs of the department holding the inquiry to be defrayed by the parties thereto) shall not apply in so far as the Secretary of State is of the opinion, having regard to the object and result of the inquiry, that his costs should be defrayed by him.

Making of order

5 After considering any objections to the order which are not withdrawn and, where a local inquiry is held, the report of the person who held the inquiry, the

Secretary of State may make the order either without modification or subject to such modifications as he thinks fit.

Special parliamentary procedure

6 If any objection is duly made by a person required to be furnished with a copy of the draft order and is not withdrawn, the order shall be subject to special parliamentary procedure.

SCHEDULE 6

Section 122(1).

ROADS WITH SPECIAL ENGINEERING DIFFICULTIES

Introductory

1 In this Schedule a "road with special engineering difficulties" means a road for the time being designated under section 122 as having special engineering difficulties.

Requirement of plan and section

2 (1) In a road with special engineering difficulties road works (other than emergency works) involving—

(a) breaking up or opening the road, or any sewer, drain or tunnel under it, or

(b) tunnelling or boring under the road,

shall not be executed until a plan and section of the works have been settled by agreement between the undertaker and each of the relevant authorities or by arbitration.

(2) For that purpose an undertaker proposing to execute any such works shall submit a plan and section of them to each relevant authority.

3 Emergency works may be executed without a plan and section being so submitted or settled, but as soon as is reasonably practicable after the execution of the works the undertaker shall furnish a plan and section of the works to each relevant authority.

4 (1) In the case of a road which is not a public road and which the road managers have no liability to the public to maintain or repair, the undertaker may give the road managers a notice stating—

(a) the general effect of the works proposed or, as the case may be, of the emergency works executed, and

(b) that it is a notice given for the purposes of this paragraph.

(2) Where such a notice is given paragraphs 2 and 3 do not apply if the road managers do not, within 10 working days from the date on which the notice was given to them, give notice to the undertaker requiring the submission or furnishing of a plan and section to them.

5 (1) A relevant authority to whom a plan and section of works are required to be submitted or furnished may accept as, or in lieu of, a plan and section any description of the works, whether in diagram form or not, which appears to them to be sufficient.

(2) References in this Schedule to a plan and section include any such description so submitted or furnished to the form of which the relevant authority have not objected within the time allowed under paragraph 7(2) below.

6 If an undertaker—

(a) executes any works in contravention of paragraph 2, or

(b) fails to furnish a plan and section in accordance with paragraph 3,

he commits an offence and is liable on summary conviction to a fine not exceeding level 3 on the standard scale.

Procedure on submission of plan and section

7 (1) A relevant authority to whom there is submitted a plan and section of road works proposed to be executed in a road with special engineering difficulties shall give notice to the undertaker—

(a) approving the plan and section without modification, or

(b) objecting to them in form as being on too small a scale or giving insufficient particulars, or

(c) approving them subject to modifications specified in the notice, or

(d) disapproving them.

(2) The notice shall be given without avoidable delay, and at the latest before the end of the period of—

(a) 7 working days in the case of a plan and section of works relating only to—

(i) a service pipe or service line, or

(ii) overhead electric lines or telecommunication apparatus, and

(b) one month in any other case;

and as between the undertaker and a relevant authority who do not duly give notice before the end of that period, the plan and section as submitted shall be deemed to have been settled by agreement.

(3) The reference in sub-paragraph (2)(a)(i) to a service pipe or service line is to—

(a) a pipe or line through or by means of which a supply of gas, electricity or water is afforded or intended to be afforded to premises—

(i) directly from premises from which the supply originates, or

(ii) from a main, that is, a pipe or line for affording a general supply;

(b) a pipe through or by means of which sewerage services are afforded, or intended to be afforded, which is not a sewer vested in a local authority; or

(c) underground telecommunication apparatus for the purpose of providing a service by means of a telecommunication system to or from particular premises (as opposed to apparatus for the general purposes of such a system).

But so much of any such pipe, line or apparatus as is placed, or intended to be placed, for a continuous length of 100 metres or more in a public road shall be treated as not being a service pipe or service line.

(4) In this paragraph—

"electric line" has the same meaning as in Part I of the Electricity Act 1989;

"telecommunication apparatus" has the same meaning as in Schedule 2 to the Telecommunications Act 1984; and "telecommunication system" has the meaning given by section 4(1) of that Act (read with subsection (2) of that section).

8 (1) Where a relevant authority give notice approving the plan and section subject to modifications, or disapproving the plan and section, they shall state their reasons for doing so.

(2) If a relevant authority duly give notice—

(a) objecting to the plan and section in form, or

(b) approving them subject to modifications to which the undertaker does not agree, or

(c) disapproving them,

then, unless the notice is withdrawn, the undertaker may refer the matter to arbitration.

(3) If the notice is withdrawn, the plan and section as submitted be deemed to have been settled by agreement between them and the undertaker.

9 A local authority in whom a sewer is vested or a bridge authority may not give notice—

(a) approving a plan and section subject to modifications, or

(b) disapproving a plan and section,

on grounds other than such as relate to the injurious effect of the proposed works on their sewer or, as the case may be, on the structure or stability of their bridge.

Settlement of plan and section by arbitration

10 (1) The duty of the arbiter where a matter is referred to arbitration is to settle a plan and section of works of the kind proposed, as works to be executed in the road.

(2) He may require the undertaker to submit to him a plan and section in such form, require the relevant authority to submit to him such observations on a plan and section submitted to him, and require the undertaker or the relevant authority to furnish him with such information and to take such other steps, as appear to him to be requisite.

(3) He may treat compliance with any such requirement made of the undertaker as a condition of his proceeding with the settlement of a plan and section, and compliance with any such requirement made of the relevant authority as a condition of his settling a plan and section otherwise than as proposed by the undertaker.

11 (1) Where the reference relates to the placing, altering or changing the position of apparatus in a road which is carried by or goes under a bridge, then, if the arbiter is satisfied—

(a) that the execution of the works would be likely to affect injuriously the structure or stability of the bridge, and

(b) that it is not practicable to meet objection on that ground to the plan and section submitted,

he shall so declare, and shall not settle any plan and section of those works on the reference.

(2) This does not affect the right of the undertaker to submit another plan and section.

Objection to works executed without plan and section being settled

12 (1) This paragraph applies where road works have been executed in a road with special engineering difficulties without a plan and section having been settled with the road works authority or another relevant authority, whether the works were executed in contravention of paragraph 2 above or were emergency works.

(2) The authority in question may, by notice to the undertaker, object to any of the works; and after affording the undertaker an opportunity to enter into an agreement with them for meeting the objection, may refer the matter to arbitration.

(3) The arbiter may direct the alteration of the works to conform to a plan and section settled by him, or the removal of any apparatus placed in the execution of the works, and the undertaker shall comply with any such direction.

(4) In settling the terms of any such direction the arbiter shall satisfy himself that compliance with it will not involve any undue interruption or restriction of the supply or service for the purposes of which the works were executed.

(5) If an undertaker fails to execute works in accordance with a direction under this paragraph, he commits an offence and is liable on summary conviction to a fine not exceeding level 3 on the standard scale.

Execution of works in accordance with plan and section

13 (1) An undertaker executing road works in a road with special engineering difficulties shall, where a plan and section have been settled, execute the works in accordance with the plan and section as settled, or, if each of the relevant authorities agrees to the modification of the plan or section, in accordance with them as so modified.

(2) If an undertaker fails to comply with sub-paragraph (1) he commits an offence and is liable on summary conviction to a fine not exceeding level 3 on the standard scale.

SCHEDULE 7

Sections 160(4) and 161(6).

PROCEDURE FOR MAKING CERTAIN ORDERS UNDER PART IV

Publication of proposals

1 Where the Secretary of State proposes to make an order under section 160 (effect of Part IV on certain existing special enactments or instruments), or an order under section 161 (effect of Part IV on other existing enactments or instruments) relating to a special enactment or instrument, he shall publish in the Edinburgh Gazette, and in at least one newspaper circulating in the area in relation to which the enactment or instrument in question has effect, a notice—

(a) stating the general effect of the proposed order,

(b) specifying a place in that area where a copy of the draft order may be inspected by any person free of charge at all reasonable hours or may be purchased by any person at a reasonable charge, and

(c) stating that any person may, by notice given to the Secretary of State within three months from the date of the publication of the notice, object to the proposed order.

Notice to parties affected

2 Not later than the day on which the notice is published or, if it is published on two or more days, the day on which it is first published, the Secretary of State shall furnish each of the parties specified below by reference to the nature of the order with a copy of the draft order.

Order under section 160(4)(a) relating to protection afforded by an enactment or instrument	The undertaker by whom the power is exercisable and each of the persons to whom the protection in question was afforded.
Order under section 160(4)(b) relating to requirement of consent	The person whose consent would be required and the undertaker who would be required to obtain the consent.
Order under section 160(4)(c) rendering condition valid	The person by whom the condition would be imposed and the undertakers who would be required to comply with it.
Order under section 160(4)(d) modifying enactment or instrument to remove uncertainty or obscurity	As indicated above, according to whether the order relates to the protection afforded by an enactment or instrument, a consent requirement or the validity of a condition.
Order under section 161 amending, repealing or preserving effect of enactment or instrument	Any person whose interests are specially affected by the proposed provision.

Local inquiry

3 (1) The Secretary of State shall cause a local inquiry to be held if an objection to the proposed order is received by him—

(a) from a person required to be furnished with a copy of the draft order within three months from the date of his being furnished therewith, or

(b) from any other person appearing to him to be affected within three months from the day on which the notice of the proposed order is published, or if it is published on two or more days from the later or latest of them,

and the objection is not withdrawn.

(2) In the case of an objection made otherwise than by a person required to be furnished with a copy of the draft order, the Secretary of State may dispense with such an inquiry if he is satisfied that it is unnecessary.

4 (1) If the Secretary of State so directs, an inquiry under paragraph 3 shall be held by Commissioners under the Private Legislation Procedure (Scotland) Act 1936.

(2) A direction under this paragraph is deemed to have been given under section 2 of the Statutory Orders (Special Procedure) Act 1945, as read with section 10 of that Act, and the provisions of that Act with regard to the publication of notices in the Edinburgh Gazette shall, notwithstanding anything contained in that Act, not apply to any order under section 160 which is subject to special parliamentary procedure.

(3) If the Secretary of State does not give a direction under this paragraph, the provisions of section 210(2) to (8) of the Local Government (Scotland) Act 1973 (which relate to the giving of evidence at, and the defraying of costs of, inquiries) apply in relation to a local inquiry held under paragraph 3.

Making of order

5 After considering any objections to the order which are not withdrawn and, where a local inquiry is held, the report of the person who held the inquiry, the Secretary of State may make the order either without modification or subject to such modifications as he thinks fit.

Special parliamentary procedure

6 If any objection is duly made by a person required to be furnished with a copy of the draft order and is not withdrawn, the order shall be subject to special parliamentary procedure.

SCHEDULE 8

Section 168(1).

MINOR AND CONSEQUENTIAL AMENDMENTS

PART I

AMENDMENTS OF THE HIGHWAYS ACT 1980

1 In section 139 of the Highways Act 1980 (control of builders' skips), in subsection (11) (definition of "builder's skip" and "owner") for "and section 140" substitute ", section 140 and section 140A".

2 After section 140 of the Highways Act 1980, insert—

"140A "Builders" skips: charge for occupation of highway

"140A "140A "Builders" skips: charge for occupation of highway

(1) The Minister may make provision by regulations requiring the owner of a builder's skip deposited on a highway maintainable at the public expense to pay a charge to the highway authority where—

(a) the period for which the skip remains in the highway exceeds such period as may be prescribed, and

(b) the skip is not removed within a reasonable period.

(2) For this purpose "a reasonable period" means such period as is agreed by the authority and the owner of the skip to be reasonable or, in default of such agreement, is determined by arbitration to be reasonable in the circumstances.

In default of agreement, the authority's view as to what is a reasonable period shall be acted upon pending the decision of the arbitrator.

(3) The regulations may provide that if a person applying to the highway authority for permission under section 139 above submits together with his application an estimate of the likely duration of the occupation of the highway, the period stated in the estimate shall be taken to be agreed by the authority to be reasonable unless they give notice, in such manner and within such period as may be prescribed, objecting to the estimate.

(4) The regulations may also provide that if it appears to the owner of the skip that by reason of matters not previously foreseen or reasonably foreseeable the duration of the occupation of the highway—

(a) is likely to exceed the prescribed period,

(b) is likely to exceed the period stated in his previous estimate, or

(c) is likely to exceed the period previously agreed or determined to be a reasonable period,

he may submit an estimate or revised estimate accordingly, and that if he does so any previous estimate, agreement or determination shall cease to have effect and the period stated in the new estimate shall be taken to be agreed by the authority to be reasonable unless they give notice, in such manner and within such period as may be prescribed, objecting to the estimate.

(5) The amount of the charge shall be determined in such manner as may be prescribed by reference to the period for which the highway is occupied by the skip and the extent of the occupation.

Different rates of charge may be prescribed according to the place and time of the occupation and such other factors as appear to the Minister to be relevant.

(6) The regulations may make provision as to the time and manner of making payment of any charge.

(7) The regulations shall provide that a highway authority may reduce the amount, or waive payment, of a charge in any particular case, in such classes of case as they may decide or as may be prescribed, or generally.

(8) In this section "prescribed" means prescribed by the Minister by regulations.".

3 In section 144 of the Highways Act 1980 (power to erect flagpoles, &c. on highways), in subsection (6), in the definition of "statutory undertakers" for the words from "any person entitled" to "section 181 below" substitute "any licensee under a street works licence".

4 In section 169 of the Highways Act 1980 (control of scaffolding on highways), in the closing words of subsection (4) (which relate to the meaning of "statutory undertakers") for the words from "any person entitled" to "section 181 below" substitute "any licensee under a street works licence".

5 In section 170 of the Highways Act 1980 (control of mixing mortar, &c. on highways), in subsection (2)(e) for the words from "a person entitled" to "section 181 below" substitute "any licensee under a street works licence".

6 After section 171 of the Highways Act 1980 (control of deposit of building materials, &c.) insert—

"171A Works under s. 169 or s. 171: charge for occupation of the highway

"171A "171A Works under s. 169 or s. 171: charge for occupation of the highway

(1) The Minister may make provision by regulations requiring a person carrying out any of the following works in a highway maintainable at the public expense—

(a) erecting or retaining a relevant structure within the meaning of section 169(1) above, or

(b) depositing building materials, rubbish or other things, or making a temporary excavation, as mentioned in section 171(1) above,

to pay a charge to the highway authority if the duration of the works exceeds such period as may be prescribed and the works are not completed within a reasonable period.

(2) For this purpose "a reasonable period" means such period as is agreed by the authority and the person executing the works to be reasonable or, in default of such agreement, is determined by arbitration to be reasonable in the circumstances.

In default of agreement, the authority's view as to what is a reasonable period shall be acted upon pending the decision of the arbitrator.

(3) The regulations may provide that if a person applying to the highway authority for a licence under section 169 or consent under section 171 submits together with his application an estimate of the likely duration of the works, the period stated in the estimate shall be taken to be agreed by the authority to be reasonable unless they give notice, in such manner and within such period as may be prescribed, objecting to the estimate.

(4) The regulations may also provide that if it appears to the person carrying out the works that by reason of matters not previously foreseen or reasonably foreseeable the duration of the works—

(a) is likely to exceed the prescribed period,

(b) is likely to exceed the period stated in his previous estimate, or

(c) is likely to exceed the period previously agreed or determined to be a reasonable period,

he may submit an estimate or revised estimate accordingly, and that if he does so any previous estimate, agreement or determination shall cease to have effect and the period stated in the new estimate shall be taken to be agreed by the authority to be reasonable unless they give notice, in such manner and within such period as may be prescribed, objecting to the estimate.

(5) The amount of the charge shall be determined in such manner as may be prescribed by reference to the time taken to complete the works and the extent to which the surface of the highway is affected by the works.

Different rates of charge may be prescribed according to the description of works, the place and time at which they are executed and such other factors as appear to the Minister to be relevant.

(6) The regulations may make provision as to the time and manner of making payment of any charge.

(7) The regulations shall provide that a highway authority may reduce the amount, or waive payment, of a charge in any particular case, in such classes of case as they may decide or as may be prescribed, or generally.

(8) In this section "prescribed" means prescribed by the Minister by regulations.".

7 In section 174 of the Highways Act 1980 (precautions to be taken by persons executing works in streets), in subsection (1) for the words from the beginning to "executing works in any street he" substitute—

"Where a person is executing works of any description in a street (other than street works within the meaning of Part III of the New Roads and Street Works Act 1991), he".

8 In section 179 of the Highways Act 1980 (control of construction of cellars, &c. under the street), in subsection (7) for the words from "code-regulated works" to the end substitute "street works within the meaning of Part III of the New Roads and Street Works Act 1991".

9 In section 184 of the Highways Act 1980 (vehicle crossings over footways and verges), omit—

(a) in subsection (9), the words from "In relation to works" to the end, and

(b) subsection (14);and in subsection (15) (supplementary provision as to costs recoverable by highway authority), for "the cost of any works which are required by the said Act of 1950 to be executed" substitute "the cost of any measures needing to be taken in relation to undertaker's apparatus, in accordance with section 84 of the New Roads and Street Works Act 1991,".

10 In section 285 of the Highways Act 1980 (power of Minister to execute certain road improvements), in subsection (6) (provisions for purposes of which Minister to be treated as acting as agent of local highway authority) for "the Public Utilities Street Works Act 1950" substitute "Part III of the New Roads and Street Works Act 1991".

11 In section 290 of the Highways Act 1980 (supplementary provisions as to entry for purposes of survey), for subsection (8) substitute—

"(8) Where in the exercise of a power conferred by section 289 above works authorised by subsection (3) of that section are to be executed in a street—

(a) section 55 of the New Roads and Street Works Act 1991 (notice of starting date of works), so far as it requires notice to be given to a person having apparatus in the street which is likely to be affected by the works,

(b) section 69 of that Act (requirements to be complied with where works likely to affect another person's apparatus in the street), and

(c) section 82 of that Act (liability for damage or loss caused),

have effect in relation to the works as if they were street works within the meaning of Part III of that Act.".

12 In section 292 of the Highways Act 1980 (compensation for damage resulting from exercise of powers of entry, &c.), in subsection (2) (avoidance of double

compensation) for "section 26 of the Public Utilities Street Works Act 1950" substitute "section 82 of the New Roads and Street Works Act 1991".

13 In section 314 of the Highways Act 1980 (offences by bodies corporate), in subsection (3) for "177 and 181" substitute "and 177".

14 In section 325 of the Highways Act 1980 (provisions as to regulations, schemes and orders), in subsection (2)(a) (regulations subject to annulment) after "section 257(4) above" insert "or such regulations as are mentioned in subsection (2A) below"; and after that subsection insert—

"(2A) A statutory instrument containing—

(a) the first regulations for the purposes of section 140A,

(b) the first regulations for the purposes of section 171A as it applies in relation to erecting or retaining a relevant structure within the meaning of section 169(1) above, or

(c) the first regulations for the purposes of section 171A as it applies in relation to depositing building materials, rubbish or other things, or making a temporary excavation, as mentioned in section 171(1) above,shall not be made unless a draft of them has been laid before and approved by a resolution of each House of Parliament.".

15 (1) Section 329(1) of the Highways Act 1980 (interpretation) is amended as follows.

(2) For the definition of "street" substitute—

""street" has the same meaning as in Part III of the New Roads and Street Works Act 1991;".

(3) At the appropriate place insert—

""street works licence" means a licence under section 50 of the New Roads and Street Works Act 1991, and "licensee" in relation to such a licence, has the meaning given by subsection (3) of that section;".

16 (1) Section 334 of the Highways Act 1980 (savings for British Telecommunications) is amended as follows.

(2) In subsection (6) for "authority's works as defined in Part II of the Public Utilities Street Works Act 1950" substitute "major highway works, major bridge works or major transport works within the meaning of Part III of the New Roads and Street Works Act 1991".

(3) In subsection (9) for the words from "the code" to "thereby affected)" substitute "the provisions of Part III of the New Roads and Street Works Act 1991 relating to major highway works, major bridge works or major transport works".

PART II

AMENDMENTS OF THE ROAD TRAFFIC REGULATION ACT 1984

Traffic regulation orders outside Greater London

17 (1) Section 1 of the Road Traffic Regulation Act 1984 is amended as follows.

(2) In subsection (1) for the words from the beginning to "London" substitute "The traffic authority for a road outside Greater London may make an order under this section (referred to in this Act as a "traffic regulation order") in respect of the road"

(3) Omit subsection (2) (authorities having power to make orders).

(4) For subsection (3) substitute—

"(3) A traffic regulation order made by a local traffic authority may, with the consent of the Secretary of State, extend to a road in relation to which he is the traffic authority if the order forms part of a scheme of general traffic control relating to roads of which at least one has a junction with the length of road in question.".

(5) Omit subsections (4) and (5) (which provide that the power is not exercisable in relation to a special road).

18 (1) Section 2 of the Road Traffic Regulation Act 1984 (what a traffic regulation order may provide) is amended as follows.

(2) In subsection (1) for the words from the beginning to "of this Act)" substitute "A traffic regulation order may make".

(3) In subsection (2) for the words from the beginning to "that subsection" substitute "The provision that may be made by a traffic regulation order".

(4) In subsection (4) for the words from the beginning to "may include" substitute "A local traffic authority may include".

19 In section 3(1) of the Road Traffic Regulation Act 1984 (restrictions on traffic regulation orders) omit the words from the beginning to "of this Act".

20 In section 5 of the Road Traffic Regulation Act 1984 (contravention of traffic regulation order), omit subsection (2).

Orders as to traffic regulation in Greater London

21 (1) Section 6 of the Road Traffic Regulation Act 1984 (orders as to traffic regulation in Greater London) is amended as follows.

(2) In subsection (1) for the words from the beginning to "foregoing words)" substitute—

"The traffic authority for a road in Greater London may make an order under this section for controlling or regulating vehicular and other traffic (including pedestrians).Provision may, in particular, be made—".

(3) For subsection (2) substitute—

"(2) In the case of a road for which the Secretary of State is the traffic authority, the power to make an order under this section is also exercisable, with his consent, by the local traffic authority.".

(4) Omit subsection (4) (which provides that the power is not exercisable in relation to a special road).

(5) In subsection (6) omit the words from "and in subsection (4)" to the end.

22 In section 8 of the Road Traffic Regulation Act 1984 (contravention of order under s.6), omit subsection (2).

Experimental traffic schemes

23 (1) Section 9 of the Road Traffic Regulation Act 1984 (experimental traffic orders) is amended as follows.

(2) For subsection (1) substitute—

"(1) The traffic authority for a road may, for the purposes of carrying out an experimental scheme of traffic control, make an order under this section (referred to in this Act as an "experimental traffic order") making any such provision—

(a) as respects a road outside Greater London, as may be made by a traffic regulation order;

(b) as respects a road in Greater London, as may be made by an order under section 6, 45, 46, 49, 83(2) or 84 of this Act.".

(3) For subsection (2) substitute—

"(2) An experimental traffic order made by a local traffic authority outside Greater London may, with the consent of the Secretary of State, extend to a road in relation to which he is the traffic authority if the order forms part of a scheme of general traffic control relating to roads of which at least one has a junction with the length of road in question.

(2A) In the case of a road in Greater London for which the Secretary of State is the traffic authority, the power to make an order under this section is also exercisable, with his consent, by the local traffic authority.".

(4) After subsection (5) insert—

"(5A) So much of section 4(1) or 7(1) of this Act as provides for a presumption that a traffic sign is lawfully placed shall apply for the purposes of an order under this section making any such provision as is referred to in that subsection.".

24 (1) Section 10 of the Road Traffic Regulation Act 1984 (supplementary provisions as to experimental traffic orders) is amended as follows.

(2) For subsection (2) substitute—

"(2) An experimental traffic order may include provision empowering a specified officer of the authority who made the order, or a person authorised by such a specified officer, to modify or suspend the operation of the order or any provision of it if it appears to him essential—

(a) in the interests of the expeditious, convenient and safe movement of traffic,

(b) in the interests of providing suitable and adequate on-street parking facilities, or

(c) for preserving or improving the amenities of the area through which any road affected by the order runs.

The power conferred by such a provision shall be exercised only after consulting the appropriate chief officer of police and giving such public notice as the Secretary of State may direct.".

(3) For subsection (3) substitute—

"(3) Any such power to modify an experimental traffic order as is mentioned in subsection (2) above does not extend to making additions to the order or to designating additional on-street parking places for which charges are made; but subject to that the modifications may be of any description.".

25 In section 12 of the Road Traffic Regulation Act 1984 (experimental traffic schemes in Greater London), for subsection (2) substitute—

"(1A) The local authority shall not give their consent to any such scheme affecting a road for which the Secretary of State is the traffic authority except with his agreement.

(2) The Secretary of State may in the case of any scheme, after consultation with the local authority, direct them to consent to the scheme within a specified period or to withhold their consent.".

Temporary prohibition or restriction of traffic

26 (1) Section 14 of the Road Traffic Regulation Act 1984 (temporary prohibition or restriction of traffic on roads) is amended as follows.

(2) For subsections (1) and (2) (power to make orders) substitute—

"(1) If the traffic authority for a road are satisfied that traffic on the road should be restricted or prohibited—

(a) by reason that works are being or are proposed to be executed on or near the road, or

(b) by reason of the likelihood of danger to the public or of serious damage to the road,

the authority may by order restrict or prohibit temporarily the use of the road, or any part of it, by vehicles, or by vehicles of any class, or by pedestrians, to such extent and subject to such conditions or exceptions as they may consider necessary.

(2) A traffic authority when considering the question of the making of an order under subsection (1) shall have regard to the existence of alternative routes suitable for the traffic which will be affected by the order.".

(3) For subsection (3) (power to issue notice) substitute—

"(3) The traffic authority for a road may at any time by notice restrict or prohibit temporarily the use of the road, or any part of it, by vehicles, or by vehicles of any class, or by pedestrians, where, owing to the likelihood of danger to the public or of serious damage to the road, it appears to them necessary that such a restriction or prohibition should come into force without delay.".

(4) In subsection (3A) (power to make order or issue notice for purposes of clearing litter or cleaning)—

(a) for "highway or roads authority" substitute "traffic authority", and

(b) for "highway or road" substitute "road".

(5) For subsection (5) substitute—

"(5) Where a traffic authority ("the initiating authority") make an order under subsection (1) or issue a notice under subsection (3), any such provision as is described in any of paragraphs (a) to (c) of section 2(2) or in section 2(3) of this Act may be made as respects any alternative road by an order made—

(a) in a case where the initiating authority are the traffic authority for the alternative road, by that authority;

(b) in any other case—

(i) where the traffic authority for the alternative road is a local traffic authority, by the initiating authority with the consent of that authority;

(ii) where the traffic authority for the alternative road is the Secretary of State, by him on the application of the initiating authority.".

27 In section 16 of the Road Traffic Regulation Act 1984 (supplementary provisions as to orders and notices under s.14), omit subsections (3) and (4).

Traffic regulation on special roads

28 (1) Section 17 of the Road Traffic Regulation Act 1984 (traffic regulation on special roads) is amended as follows.

(2) For subsection (1) (traffic authorised to use special road) substitute—

"(1) A special road shall not be used except by traffic of a class authorised to do so—

(a) in England and Wales, by a scheme made, or having effect as if made, under section 16 of the Highways Act 1980 or by virtue of paragraph 3 of Schedule 23 to that Act, or

(b) in Scotland, by a scheme made, or having effect as if made, under section 7 of the Roads (Scotland) Act 1984.".

(3) In subsection (2) (regulations as to use of special roads), for the words from "and such regulations" to the end of paragraph (a) substitute—

"Such regulations may, in particular—

(a) regulate the manner in which and the conditions subject to which special roads may be used by traffic authorised to do so;".

(4) For subsection (5) (provisions as to date of opening of special road) substitute—

"(5) The provisions of this section and of any regulations under subsection (2) above do not apply in relation to a road, or part of a road, until the date declared by the traffic authority, by notice published in the prescribed manner, to be the date on which the road or part is open for use as a special road.

This does not prevent the making of regulations under subsection (2) above before that date, so as to come into force in relation to that road or part on that date.".

(5) In subsection (6) omit the words from "and "the date of opening"" to the end.

29 After section 17 of the Road Traffic Regulation Act 1984 insert—

"17A Further provisions as to special roads

"17A "17A Further provisions as to special roads

(1) On the date declared by the traffic authority, by notice published in the prescribed manner, to be the date on which a special road, or a part of a special road, is open for use as a special road, any existing order under section 1, 6, 9 or 84 of this Act relating to that road or part shall cease to have effect.

(2) This is without prejudice to any power to make orders under those provisions in relation to the road or part as a special road; and any such power may be exercised before the date referred to above, so as to take effect on that date.

(3) The procedure for making an order applies in such a case with such modifications as may be prescribed.".

Traffic regulation in other special cases

30 In section 18 of the Road Traffic Regulation Act 1984 (one-way traffic on trunk roads), in subsection (1) for the words from "an order" to "directing" substitute "an order under section 10 of the Highways Act 1980 or section 5 of the Roads (Scotland) Act 1984 directing".

31 (1) Section 19 of the Road Traffic Regulation Act 1984 (regulation of use of highways by public service vehicles) is amended as follows.

(2) In subsection (1) (making of orders by local authority), for the words from the beginning to the end of paragraph (b) substitute—

"(1) A local traffic authority outside Greater London may make orders—

(a) for determining the highways or, in Scotland, roads in their area which may or may not be used by public service vehicles;

(b) for fixing stands for public service vehicles on such highways or roads;".

(3) Omit subsection (3).

32 In section 20 of the Road Traffic Regulation Act 1984 (prohibition or restriction on use of vehicles on roads of certain classes), for subsection (3) (exclusion of provisions in relation to special roads) substitute—

"(3) No order under this section shall be made or apply in relation to a special road on or after the date declared by the traffic authority, by notice published in the prescribed manner, to be the date on which the special road, or the relevant part of the special road, is open for use as a special road.".

33 In section 21 of the Road Traffic Regulation Act 1984 (permit for trailer to carry excess weight), for subsection (3) (definition of "appropriate authority") substitute—

"(3) The appropriate authority for the purposes of this section is—

(a) in relation to a bridge for the maintenance of which a bridge authority is responsible, or a road passing over such a bridge, the bridge authority;

(b) in relation to any other road, the traffic authority and any other person responsible for the maintenance of the road.".

34 (1) Section 22 of the Road Traffic Regulation Act 1984 (traffic regulation for special areas in the countryside) is amended as follows.

(2) For subsections (3) and (4) (powers of Secretary of State as to making of orders) substitute—

"(3) The Countryside Commission, the Countryside Council for Wales and the Countryside Commission for Scotland may each make submissions to the Secretary of State as to the desirability of a traffic regulation order being made in relation to a road to which this section applies, whether or not it is a road for which he is the traffic authority.

(4) Where such a submission is made as respects a road for which he is not the traffic authority, and the traffic authority for the road notify him that they do not intend to make an order, the Secretary of State may by order under this subsection make any such provision as he might have made by a traffic regulation order if he had been the traffic authority.

This Act applies to such an order as to an order made by him in relation to a road for which he is the traffic authority.".

(3) On the coming into force of Part I of the Natural Heritage (Scotland) Act 1991, for the reference in subsection (3) as amended by this paragraph to the Countryside Commission for Scotland there shall be substituted a reference to Scottish Natural Heritage.

Pedestrian crossings

35 (1) Section 23 of the Road Traffic Regulation Act 1984 is amended as follows.

(2) For subsection (1) (power to establish pedestrian crossings) substitute—

"(1) A local traffic authority may establish crossings for pedestrians on roads for which they are the traffic authority, and may alter or remove any such crossings.

The crossings shall be indicated in the manner prescribed by regulations under section 25 of this Act.".

(3) In subsections (2) and (3) for "local authority" substitute "local traffic authority".

(4) Omit subsection (5).

36 In section 24 of the Road Traffic Regulation Act 1984 (pedestrian crossings on trunk roads), for the words from the beginning to "such crossings" substitute "The Secretary of State shall establish on roads for which he is the traffic authority such crossings", and for "and to execute" substitute "and execute".

Street playgrounds

37 For sections 29 and 30 of the Road Traffic Regulation Act 1984 (street playgrounds) substitute—

"29 Power to prohibit traffic on roads to be used as playgrounds

"29 "29 Power to prohibit traffic on roads to be used as playgrounds

(1) For the purpose of enabling a road for which they are the traffic authority to be used as a playground for children, a local traffic authority may make an order prohibiting or restricting the use of the road by vehicles, or by vehicles of any specified class, either generally or on particular days or during particular hours.

The prohibition or restriction may be subject to such exceptions and conditions as to occasional use or otherwise as may be specified in the order.

(2) An order under this section shall make provision for permitting reasonable access to premises situated on or adjacent to the road.

(3) A person who uses a vehicle or causes or permits a vehicle to be used, in contravention of an order in force under this section shall be guilty of an offence.".

38 In section 31 of the Road Traffic Regulation Act 1984 (byelaws with respect to roads used as playgrounds), in subsection (1), for the words from "by a local authority" to "have power to" substitute "under section 29 of this Act, the local traffic authority may".

Parking places

39 In section 32 of the Road Traffic Regulation Act 1984 (power of local authorities to provide parking places), in subsection (4)(a) (meaning of "local authority") for "the local roads authority" substitute "a regional or islands council".

40 In section 34 of the Road Traffic Regulation Act 1984 (provision of access to premises through off-street parking place), in subsection (1)—

(a) in the opening words omit the words "in England or Wales", and

(b) for paragraph (a) substitute—

"(a) that it would relieve or prevent congestion of traffic on a highway or, in Scotland, a road if use were made of the parking place to provide a means of access from the highway or road to premises adjoining, or abutting on, the parking place, and".

41 (1) Section 37 of the Road Traffic Regulation Act 1984 (extension of powers for purposes of general scheme of traffic control) is amended as follows.

(2) For subsection (1) substitute—

"(1) This section applies to an order made under both section 1 and section 32 of this Act by—

(a) the council of a county or metropolitan district in England and Wales, or

(b) by a regional or islands council in Scotland,

where the order is, and is stated to be, made by virtue of this section and for the purposes of a general scheme of traffic control in a stated area.".

(3) In subsection (3) for "a trunk road" substitute "a road for which the Secretary of State is the traffic authority".

42 In section 38 of the Road Traffic Regulation Act 1984 (parking place to be used as bus or coach station), in subsection (3) for "street" substitute "road".

43 In section 43 of the Road Traffic Regulation Act 1984 (control of off-street parking in Greater London) in subsection (14), in the definition of "public off-street parking place", for "parking space for motor vehicles off the highway" substitute "off-street parking accommodation" and for "space" substitute "accommodation".

44 (1) Section 45 of the Road Traffic Regulation Act 1984 (designation of paying parking places on highways) is amended as follows.

(2) For subsection (1) (power to make orders) substitute—

"(1) A local authority may by order designate parking places on highways or, in Scotland, roads in their area for vehicles or vehicles of any class specified in the order; and the authority may make charges (of such amount as may be prescribed under section 46 below) for vehicles left in a parking place so designated.

The exercise of this power by a local authority outside Greater London in relation to a highway or road for which they are not the traffic authority is subject to obtaining the consent of the traffic authority.".

(3) In subsection (3)(c) (matters to be taken into account in making orders), for the words from "parking accommodation" to "highways" or, in Scotland, "roads" substitute "off-street parking accommodation, whether in the open or under cover,".

(4) In subsection (7) (meaning of "local authority"), in paragraph (c) for "local roads authority" substitute "regional or islands council".

45 In section 53(1) of the Road Traffic Regulation Act 1984, for "highways" or, in Scotland, "roads" substitute "highways or, in Scotland, roads".

46 (1) Section 55 of the Road Traffic Regulation Act 1984 (financial provisions relating to designation orders) is amended as follows.

(2) In subsection (4)(b) and (c) for the words from "parking accommodation" to the end substitute "off-street parking accommodation, whether in the open or under cover;".

(3) For subsection (4)(d) substitute—

"(d) if it appears to the local authority that the provision in their area of further off-street parking accommodation is unnecessary or undesirable, the following purposes—

(i) meeting costs incurred, whether by the local authority or by some other person, in the provision or operation of, or of facilities for, public passenger transport services, and

(ii) the purposes of a highway or road improvement project in the local authority's area.".

(4) After subsection (4) insert—

"(4A) For the purposes of subsection (4)(d)(ii)—

(a) a highway improvement project means a project connected with the carrying out by the appropriate highway authority (whether the local authority or not) of any operation which constitutes the improvement (within the meaning of the Highways Act 1980) of a highway in the area of a local authority in England or Wales; and

(b) a road improvement project means a project connected with the carrying out by the appropriate roads authority (whether the local authority or not) of any operation which constitutes the improvement (within the meaning of the Roads (Scotland) Act 1984) of a road in the area of a local authority in Scotland.".

(5) Omit subsection (5).

Traffic signs

47 In section 64 of the Road Traffic Regulation Act 1984 (general provisions as to traffic signs), in subsection (4)(c)(i) and (ii) for "highway" substitute "road".

48 (1) Section 65 of the Road Traffic Regulation Act 1984 (powers and duties of highway authorities as to placing of traffic signs) is amended as follows.

(2) For subsection (1) (power to cause or permit placing of traffic signs) substitute—

"(1) The traffic authority may cause or permit traffic signs to be placed on or near a road, subject to and in conformity with such general directions as may be given by the Ministers acting jointly or such other directions as may be given by the Secretary of State.".

(2) In subsection (2) (direction by Secretary of State), for the opening words substitute—

"(2) The Secretary of State may give directions to a local traffic authority—".

49 In section 66(1) of the Road Traffic Regulation Act 1984 (traffic signs for giving effect to local traffic regulations), for "highway" (twice) substitute "road".

50 In section 67 of the Road Traffic Regulation Act 1984 (emergencies and temporary obstructions), in subsection (1) for "highway" (twice) substitute "road".

51 (1) Section 68 of the Road Traffic Regulation Act 1984 (placing of traffic signs in connection with exercise of other powers) is amended as follows.

(2) In subsection (1)(a), omit the reference to section 30.

(3) In subsections (2) and (3), for "highway authority" or, in Scotland, "roads authority", wherever occurring, substitute "traffic authority".

52 (1) Section 69 of the Road Traffic Regulation Act 1984 (placing of traffic signs in connection with exercise of other powers) is amended as follows.

(2) In subsection (1)—

(a) for "highway authority" or, in Scotland, "roads authority" substitute "traffic authority"; and

(b) for "the roads" or, in Scotland, "a road" substitute "the road".

(3) In subsection (2) for "highway authority" or, in Scotland, "roads authority" substitute "traffic authority".

(4) In subsection (3) for "highway authority" or, in Scotland, "local roads authority" substitute "local traffic authority".

53 In section 70 of the Road Traffic Regulation Act 1984 (default powers of Secretary of State), in subsection (1) for "highway authority" or, in Scotland, "local roads authority" substitute "local traffic authority".

54 In section 71 of the Road Traffic Regulation Act 1984 (power to enter land in connection with traffic signs), in subsection (1) for "highway authority" or, in Scotland, "local roads authority" substitute "local traffic authority".

55 In section 73 of the Road Traffic Regulation Act 1984 (powers of local traffic authorities in London), in subsection (1) for "which is not a trunk road" substitute "for which they are the traffic authority".

56 In section 77 of the Road Traffic Regulation Act 1984 (modifications as respects trunk roads), for the opening words substitute "In relation to a road for which the Secretary of State is the traffic authority".

57 In section 79 of the Road Traffic Regulation Act 1984 (advances by Secretary of State towards expenses of traffic signs), in subsection (5) for "highway authority" or, in Scotland, "local roads authority" substitute "local traffic authority".

58 In section 80 of the Road Traffic Regulation Act 1984 (exercise of traffic sign functions by person other than traffic authority), in subsection (1), for "highway authority" or, in Scotland, "roads authority" in both places where those expressions occur substitute "traffic authority".

59 (1) Section 82 of the Road Traffic Regulation Act 1984 (what roads are restricted roads) is amended as follows.

(2) In subsection (1) for the words from "if" to the end substitute—

"if—

(a) in England and Wales, there is provided on it a system of street lighting furnished by means of lamps placed not more than 200 yards apart;

(b) in Scotland, there is provided on it a system of carriageway lighting furnished by means of lamps placed not more than 185 metres apart and the road is of a classification or type specified for the purposes of this subsection in regulations made by the Secretary of State.".

(3) In subsection (2) for "A direction may be given" substitute "The traffic authority for a road may direct", and in paragraphs (a) and (b) for "a specified road" substitute "the road".

(4) For subsection (3) substitute—

"(3) A special road is not a restricted road for the purposes of section 81 on or after the date declared by the traffic authority, by notice published in the prescribed manner, to be the date on which the special road, or the relevant part of the special road, is open for use as a special road.".

60 (1) Section 83 of the Road Traffic Regulation Act 1984 (provisions as to directions under section 82) is amended as follows.

(2) In subsection (1), for the words from the beginning to "shall be given" substitute "A direction under section 82(2) by the Secretary of State shall be given".

(3) For subsection (2) substitute—

"(2) A direction under section 82(2) by a local traffic authority shall be given by means of an order made by the authority.".

61 In section 84 of the Road Traffic Regulation Act 1984 (speed limits on roads other than restricted roads), for subsection (2) (authority having power to make order) substitute—

"(2) The power to make an order under subsection (1) is exercisable by the traffic authority, who shall before exercising it in any case give public notice of their intention to do so.".

62 (1) Section 85 of the Road Traffic Regulation Act 1984 (traffic signs for indicating speed restrictions) is amended as follows.

(2) In subsection (1) (duty of Secretary of State), for the words from "in the case of" to "to" substitute "in the case of a road for which he is the traffic authority, to".

(3) In subsection (2) (duties of local traffic authorities), for the opening words substitute—

"In the case of any other road, it is the duty of the local traffic authority—".

(4) In subsection (3) for "local authority" substitute "local traffic authority".

(5) In subsection (4), for the words from the beginning to "on a road" substitute "Where no such system of street or carriageway lighting as is mentioned in section 82(1) is provided on a road,".

(6) In subsection (5) for the words from "such a system" to "subsection (4) above" substitute "such a system of street or carriageway lighting".

63 In section 86 of the Road Traffic Regulation Act 1984 (speed limits for particular classes of vehicles), omit subsection (4) (which relates to special roads).

64 Omit section 91 (definition of "local authority" for the purposes of Part VI).

65 (1) Section 92 of the Road Traffic Regulation Act 1984 (bollards and other obstructions outside Greater London) is amended as follows.

(2) In subsection (1) for "the highway authority or, in Scotland, the local roads authority" substitute "the traffic authority".

(3) For subsection (4) substitute—

"(4) The bollards or other obstructions authorised by an order under subsection (1) shall be placed on the road by the traffic authority, except as mentioned in section 93 below.".

66 (1) Section 93 of the Road Traffic Regulation Act 1984 (powers of Secretary of State in relation to functions under section 92) is amended as follows.

(2) For subsection (1) substitute—

"(1) Where by virtue of an order under section 92(1) the Secretary of State has power to place bollards or other obstructions at a point on a road, he may authorise or require the traffic authority for any other road leading into or crossing that road at that point to place the bollards or other obstructions on that other road.".

(3) In subsection (2) for "any authority" and in subsection (3) for "an authority" substitute "a local traffic authority".

67 (1) Section 94 of the Road Traffic Regulation Act 1984 (bollards and other obstructions in Greater London) is amended as follows.

(2) In subsection (1) (powers of Secretary of State), for "which is not a trunk road" substitute "for which he is not the traffic authority".

(3) In subsection (2) (powers of London borough council), for "which is not a trunk road and for which they are not the highway authority" substitute "for which neither they nor the Secretary of State are the traffic authority".

(4) In subsection (4)—

(a) in paragraph (a) for "any trunk road" substitute "any road for which he is the traffic authority"; and

(b) in paragraph (b) for "which is not a trunk road and for which they are the highway authority" substitute "for which they are the traffic authority" and for "highway authority", in the second place where it occurs, substitute "traffic authority".

68 In section 100(5) of the Road Traffic Regulation Act 1984 (definition of "local authority" for purposes of provisions about removal of abandoned vehicles, &c.), for paragraph (c) substitute—

"(c) in relation to Scotland, means a regional or islands council.".

69 In section 106 of the Road Traffic Regulation Act 1984 (initial experimental period for immobilisation of vehicles)—

(a) in subsection (7) (consent required for initial order), for "the authority responsible for traffic regulation in that area" substitute "the local traffic authority"; and

(b) omit subsection (8).

70 In the Road Traffic Regulation Act 1984, at the beginning of Part X (general and supplementary provisions) insert—

"121A Traffic authorities

"121A "121A Traffic authorities

(1) The Secretary of State is the traffic authority—

(a) for every highway in England and Wales for which he is the highway authority within the meaning of the Highways Act 1980, and

(b) for every road in Scotland for which he is the roads authority within the meaning of the Roads (Scotland) Act 1984.

(2) In Greater London, the council of the London borough or the Common Council of the City of London are the traffic authority for all roads in the borough or, as the case may be, in the City for which the Secretary of State is not the traffic authority.

(3) In England and Wales outside Greater London, the council of the county or metropolitan district are the traffic authority for all roads in the county or, as the case may be, the district for which the Secretary of State is not the traffic authority.

(4) In Scotland, the regional or islands council are the traffic authority in relation to all roads within their area for which the Secretary of State is not the traffic authority.

(5) In this Act "local traffic authority" means a traffic authority other than the Secretary of State.".

71 In section 122 of the Road Traffic Regulation Act 1984 (exercise of functions by local authorities), in subsection (1) for "the highway" or, in Scotland, "the road" substitute "the highway or, in Scotland, the road".

72 In section 124(2) of the Road Traffic Regulation Act 1984 (orders exercisable by statutory instrument), omit the reference to section 30.

73 In section 125(3) of the Road Traffic Regulation Act 1984 (exercise of powers in relation to boundary roads), omit the reference to section 30(1).

74 In section 130 of the Road Traffic Regulation Act 1984 (application of Act to Crown), in subsection (2)(a) for "76 to 91" substitute "76 to 90".

75 (1) Section 131 of the Road Traffic Regulation Act 1984 (application of road traffic enactments to Crown roads) is amended as follows.

(2) In subsection (2)(a) (twice), and in subsection (2)(b), for "highway authority" or, in Scotland, "roads authority" substitute "local traffic authority".

(3) In subsection (7)(b) for "a highway" or, in Scotland, "a public road" substitute "a highway or, in Scotland, a public road".

76 (1) Section 132 of the Road Traffic Regulation Act 1984 (special provisions as to certain Crown roads) is amended as follows.

(2) In subsection (5)—

(a) for "the local authority concerned" substitute "the traffic authority";

(b) for "the local authority may" substitute "the traffic authority may"; and

(c) for the words from "and any other power" to "as respects the Crown road" substitute "and any other power conferred by section 65 to give directions to a local traffic authority includes power to give the like directions to them as respects the Crown road".

(3) Omit subsection (6) (definition of "local authority concerned").

77 In section 134(2) of the Road Traffic Regulation Act 1984 (regulations excepted from obligation to consult), for "82(1)," substitute "82(1)(b),".

78 (1) Section 142(1) of the Road Traffic Regulation Act 1984 (general interpretation provisions) is amended as follows.

(2) Omit the definitions of "highway authority", "local highway authority", "local roads authority" and "roads authority".

(3) At the appropriate place insert—

""off-street parking accommodation" means parking accommodation for motor vehicles off the highway or, in Scotland, off the road;".

(4) For the definition of "road" substitute—

""road"—

(a) in England and Wales, means any length of highway or of any other road to which the public has access, and includes bridges over which a road passes, and

(b) in Scotland, has the same meaning as in the Roads (Scotland) Act 1984;".

(5) For the definition of "special road" substitute—

""special road", in England and Wales, has the same meaning as in the Highways Act 1980, and in Scotland has the same meaning as in the Roads (Scotland) Act 1984;".

(6) At the appropriate place insert—

""traffic authority" and "local traffic authority" have the meaning given by section 121A of this Act;".

79 In Schedule 3 to the Road Traffic Regulation Act 1984 (notification of temporary traffic restrictions), in paragraph 1(1) and (3), and in paragraph 3(2), for "the highway authority" substitute "the traffic authority".

80 (1) Schedule 9 to the Road Traffic Regulation Act 1984 (special provisions as to certain orders) is amended as follows.

(2) In paragraph 13(1) (orders requiring consent of Secretary of State), in paragraph (b) for "a trunk road" substitute "a road for which the Secretary of State is the traffic authority".

(3) In paragraph 20(1) (consultation before orders are made), omit the reference to section 30.

(4) In paragraphs 21 and 23(1)(a) (procedure regulations), omit the words "other than section 30 of this Act".

(5) In paragraph 24(b) (procedure regulations for certain orders) for "trunk roads" substitute "roads for which he is the traffic authority".

(6) In paragraph 25 (power to make different provision in each case and as to posting notices)—

(a) for "highway authority" or, in Scotland, "roads authority" substitute "traffic authority", and

(b) for the word "highway" in the two other places where it appears substitute the word "road".

(7) In paragraph 27(1) (variation or revocation of orders), omit the reference to section 30.

PART III

AMENDMENTS OF THE ROADS (SCOTLAND) ACT 1984

81 In section 35(2)(a) of the Roads (Scotland) Act 1984 (provision of lighting by roads authorities) for the words "Public Utilities Street Works Act 1950" substitute "Part IV of the New Roads and Street Works Act 1991".

82 In section 39(4) of the Roads (Scotland) Act 1984 (status of road humps)—

(a) for the words from "Part II" to "those roads)" substitute "section 117 of the New Roads and Street Works Act 1991 (restricting road works following substantial works for roads purposes)",
(b) for the words "section 21(1)(a) of that Act" substitute "subsection (3) of that section", and
(c) for the word "Part" substitute "section".

83 In section 56(3) of the Roads (Scotland) Act 1984 (control of works and excavations) for the words from "street works code" to "applies" substitute "provisions of Part IV of the New Roads and Street Works Act 1991 apply".

84 In section 57(5) of the Roads (Scotland) Act 1984 (dangerous works) for the words from "street works code" to "applies" substitute "provisions of Part IV of the New Roads and Street Works Act 1991 apply".

85 In section 59(6) of the Roads (Scotland) Act 1984 (control of obstructions in roads) for the words from "street works code" to "applies" substitute "provisions of Part IV of the New Roads and Street Works Act 1991 apply".

86 In section 60 of the Roads (Scotland) Act 1984 (fencing and lighting of obstructions and excavations)—
(a) in subsection (1), omit the words from "section 8" to "or to";
(b) after subsection (5) insert the following subsection—

"(6) This section shall not apply to an undertaker executing road works, within the meaning of Part IV of the New Roads and Street Works Act 1991."

87 In section 61 of the Roads (Scotland) Act 1984 (granting of permission to place and maintain etc. apparatus under a road)—
(a) at the end of subsection (1) insert "; and such permission shall be in writing",
(b) in subsection (4) for the words from "undertakers'" to the end substitute "road works within the meaning of section 107 of the New Roads and Street Works Act 1991", and
(c) at the end of subsection (5) insert "nor does it apply to apparatus in respect of which permission has been granted under section 109 of the New Roads and Street Works Act 1991 to execute road works".

88 After section 61 of the Roads (Scotland) Act 1984 there shall be inserted the following section—

"61A Charge for occupation of road

"61A "61A Charge for occupation of road

(1) The Secretary of State may make provision by regulations requiring a person who occupies a public road by doing anything to which this section applies to pay a charge to the roads authority if the duration of the occupation exceeds the longer of the following periods—
(a) such period as may be prescribed; or
(b) such period as is agreed by the authority and the person to be reasonable or, in default of such agreement, is determined by arbitration to be reasonable in the circumstances.

(2) This section applies to the occupation of a public road by doing anything which would require the consent or permission of a roads authority under any of the following provisions of this Act—

section 56 (works executed in or excavations under a public road);

section 58 (occupation of road for deposit of building materials and erection of scaffolding);

section 59 (placing or depositing anything in a road);

section 61 (placing, leaving, retaining, maintaining, repairing and reinstating apparatus in or under a public road); or

section 85 (depositing a builder's skip).

(3) For the purposes of paragraph (b) of subsection (1) above, in default of agreement, the roads authority's view as to what is a reasonable period shall be acted upon pending the decision of the arbiter.

(4) The regulations may provide that if a person applying to the roads authority for consent or permission under any of the provisions of this Act specified in subsection (2) above submits together with his application an estimate of the likely duration of the occupation, the period stated in the estimate shall be taken to be agreed by the authority to be reasonable unless they give notice, in such manner and within such period as may be prescribed, objecting to the estimate.

(5) The regulations may provide that if it appears to the person occupying the road that by reason of matters not previously foreseen or reasonably foreseeable the duration of the occupation—

(a) is likely to exceed the prescribed period,

(b) is likely to exceed the period stated in the previous estimate, or

(c) is likely to exceed the period previously agreed or determined to be a reasonable period,

he may submit an estimate or revised estimate accordingly, and that if he does so any previous estimate, agreement or determination shall cease to have effect and the period stated in the new estimate shall be taken to be agreed by the roads authority to be reasonable unless they give notice, in such manner and within such period as may be prescribed, objecting to the estimate.

(6) The amount of the charge shall be determined in such manner as may be prescribed by reference to the duration and extent of the occupation and different rates of charge may be prescribed according to the purpose of the occupation and such other factors as appear to the Secretary of State to be relevant.

(7) The regulations may make provision as to the time and manner of making payment of any charge.

(8) The regulations shall provide that a roads authority may reduce the amount, or waive payment, of a charge in any particular case, in such classes of case as they may decide or as may be prescribed, or generally.

(9) In this section "prescribed" means prescribed by the Secretary of State by regulations.".

89 In section 85 of the Roads (Scotland) Act 1984 (control of builders' skips on road), in paragraph (a) of subsection (1) after the word "the" where it first occurs insert "written".

90 In section 121(2) of the Roads (Scotland) Act 1984 (power to obtain road-making materials) for the words "Public Utilities Street Works Act 1950" substitute "Part IV of the New Roads and Street Works Act 1991".

91 In section 132(3) of the Roads (Scotland) Act 1984 (saving for operators of telecommunications code systems) for the words from "Part II" to the end of that subsection substitute "Part IV of the New Roads and Street Works Act 1991".

92 In section 135(1) of the Roads (Scotland) Act 1984 (restriction of power of local authority in whom a sewer is vested) for the words "Sections 133 and 134" substitute "Section 134".

93 In subsection (2) of section 143 of the Roads (Scotland) Act 1984 (provisions as to regulations and orders)—

(a) in sub-paragraph (ii) of paragraph (a) (orders subject to negative resolution) after the word "section" insert "8 or",

(b) in sub-paragraph (i) of paragraph (b) (orders subject to affirmative resolution) after the word "Act" insert "or regulations made for the first time under section 61A of this Act", and

(c) in sub-paragraph (ii) of paragraph (b), omit the words "8 or".

94 In section 151(1) of the Roads (Scotland) Act 1984 (interpretation)—

(a) in the definition of "proposed public road" for the words "Public Utilities Street Works Act 1950" substitute "Part IV of the New Roads and Street Works Act 1991", and

(b) in the definition of "road" after the words "whatever means" insert "and whether subject to a toll or not".

95 In section 155(d) of the Roads (Scotland) Act 1984 (general adaptation of subordinate legislation) for the words from "Schedule 2" to the end of that paragraph substitute "section 146 of the New Roads and Street Works Act 1991".

96 (1) In Schedule 1 to the Roads (Scotland) Act 1984 (procedures for making or confirming certain orders or schemes), after paragraph 14 there shall be inserted the following Part—

"Part IIA

Toll Orders Under Section 27 of the New Roads and Street Works Act 1991

14A (1) Where the Secretary of State proposes to make a toll order under section 27 of the New Roads and Street Works Act 1991, he shall prepare a draft of the order and shall publish in at least one newspaper circulating in the area in which the proposed special road is to be situated, and in the Edinburgh Gazette, a notice—

(a) stating the general effect of the proposed order;

(b) naming a place in that area where a copy of the draft order may be inspected by any person free of charge at all reasonable hours during a period specified in the notice, being a period of not less than six weeks from the date of the publication of the notice; and

(c) stating that, within that period, any person may by notice to the Secretary of State object to the making of the order.

(2) Where a toll order is submitted to the Secretary of State by a local roads authority, the authority shall publish in at least one newspaper circulating in the area in which the proposed special road is to be situated, and in the Edinburgh Gazette, a notice—

(a) stating the general effect of the order as submitted to the Secretary of State;

(b) naming a place in that area where a copy of the order may be inspected by any person free of charge at all reasonable hours during a period specified in the notice, being a period of not less than six weeks from the date of the publication of the notice; and

(c) stating that, within that period, any person may by notice to the Secretary of State object to the confirmation of the order.

(3) Where it is intended that the proposed toll order shall authorise the special road authority to assign their rights to charge and collect tolls, the Secretary of State or, as the case may be, the local roads authority shall make a statement containing such information as may be prescribed with respect to that assignation and the person to whom the rights are intended to be assigned and—

(a) the statement shall be made available for inspection with the copy of the order to which the notice under subparagraph (1) or (2) relates; and

(b) the notice shall state that such a statement will be so available.

(4) In sub-paragraph (3) "prescribed" means prescribed by the Secretary of State by regulations made by statutory instrument which shall be subject to annulment in pursuance of a resolution of either House of Parliament.

14B. The Secretary of State may, if he is satisfied that in the circumstances of the case the holding of an inquiry is unnecessary, dispense with such an inquiry.

14C (1) Subject to paragraph 19 below, after considering objections (if any) to the proposed order which are not withdrawn and, where a local inquiry is held, the report of the person who held the inquiry, the Secretary of State may make or confirm the order either without modification or subject to such modifications as he thinks fit.

(2) The power under this paragraph to make or confirm the order includes power to make or confirm it so far as relating to part of the proposals contained in it (either without modification or subject to such modifications as the Secretary of State thinks fit) while deferring consideration of the remaining part.

14D (1) A toll order shall be subject to special parliamentary procedure where—

(a) the relevant special road scheme provides for the appropriation by or transfer to the special road authority of an existing public road comprised in the route prescribed by the scheme, and

(b) the toll order authorises the charging of tolls for the use of that existing road or any part of it, unless the Secretary of State is satisfied as regards all classes of traffic entitled to use the existing road that another reasonably convenient route free of toll is available, or will be provided before the date on which the appropriation or transfer takes effect, and certifies accordingly.

(2) Where the Secretary of State proposes to give such a certificate, he shall—

(a) give public notice of his intention to do so,

(b) afford an opportunity to all persons interested to make representations and objections, and

(c) cause a public local inquiry to be held if it appears to him to be expedient to do so, having regard to representations or objections made,

and before deciding whether to give the certificate he shall consider any representations and objections made and, if an inquiry has been held, the report of the person who held the inquiry.

(3) As soon as may be after giving a certificate, the Secretary of State shall publish in the Edinburgh Gazette, and in such other manner as he thinks best for informing persons affected, a notice stating that the certificate has been given.

14E. In this Part of this Schedule "proposed order" includes an order made by a local roads authority and submitted to the Secretary of State.".

(2) In paragraph 18 of that Schedule, for the words "5 or 11" there shall be substituted the words "5, 11 or 14B".

(3) In paragraph 19 of that Schedule—

(a) in sub-paragraph (a), after "1" insert "or 14A";

(b) in sub-paragraph (b), after "above" there shall be inserted the words "or held under paragraph 14B above"; and

(c) in sub-paragraph (c), for the words "and 13" there shall be substituted the words ", 13 and 14C".

97 At the end of Schedule 2 to the Roads (Scotland) Act 1984 (validity and date of operation of certain orders and schemes), the following paragraph shall be inserted—

"(6) The provisions of paragraphs 2 to 4 above apply in relation to a certificate under paragraph 14D(1) of Schedule 1 to this Act as in relation to a scheme or order to which this Schedule applies, subject to the following modifications—

(a) the reference in paragraph 2 above to the notice required by paragraph 1 above shall be construed as a reference to the notice required by paragraph 14D(3) of that Schedule, and

(b) in paragraph 4 above for the words "made or confirmed" there shall be substituted the word "given" and the words from "and shall become operative" to the end shall be omitted.".

PART IV

AMENDMENTS OF OTHER ENACTMENTS

Roads Act 1920 (c. 72)

98 In section 10 of the Roads Act 1920 (powers of Secretary of State in relation to charges for use of vehicles on roads), at the end insert—

"Nothing in this section applies to any sum payable by virtue of Part I or II of the New Roads and Street Works Act 1991.".

Fire Services Act 1947 (c. 41)

99 (1) The Fire Services Act 1947 is amended as follows.

(2) In section 3(2) (supplementary powers of fire authorities; provisions as to exercise of power to place fire alarms in public places), for the words from the beginning to "maintaining the road;" or, in Scotland, "of the roads authority;" substitute—

"(2) Before exercising the powers conferred by subsection (1)(c) above in relation to a highway for which they are not the highway authority or, in Scotland, a public road for which they are not the roads authority, a fire authority shall obtain the consent of the highway or roads authority;".

(3) In section 38(1) (interpretation)—

(a) at the appropriate place insert—

" "highway authority" has the same meaning as in the Highways Act 1980;"; and

(b) in the definition of "road" for the words "Public Utilities Street Works Act 1950" substitute "Part IV of the New Roads and Street Works Act 1991".

Land Powers (Defence) Act 1958 (c. 30)

100 In the Land Powers (Defence) Act 1958, after section 18 insert—

"18A Modification of street works or road works provisions

"18A "18A Modification of street works or road works provisions

(1) In relation to works in exercise of the powers under a wayleave order, or the powers conferred by section 12 of the Requisitioned Land and War Works Act 1948, the provisions of Part III or IV of the New Roads and Street Works Act 1991 (street works in England and Wales or road works in Scotland) have effect subject to the provisions of this section.

(2) The provisions of Schedule 4 or 6 of that Act (settlement of plan and section for works in streets or roads with special engineering difficulties) have effect subject as follows—

(a) an objection to a plan and section in form shall be disregarded if a Minister certifies that in his opinion it would be against the national interest to submit a plan and section on a larger scale or giving further particulars;

(b) no modification of a plan and section shall be made which would involve an unacceptable diversion or change; and

(c) a plan and section shall not be disapproved on the ground that there should be such a diversion or change.

(3) An arbitrator or arbiter appointed in pursuance of—

(a) paragraph 8(3) of Schedule 4 or 6 of that Act (settlement of plan and section in case of works in street or road with special engineering difficulties), or

(b) section 84(3) or 143(3) of that Act (settlement of necessary measures in case of apparatus affected by certain major works),

shall not provide for an unacceptable diversion or change.

(4) In subsections (2) and (3) above an "unacceptable diversion or change" means—

(a) a lateral diversion of a government oil pipe-line to which the Minister on whose behalf the works are to be executed does not consent, or

(b) a change of the site of accessory works which would necessitate such a diversion.".

Pipelines Act 1962 (c. 58)

101 (1) The Pipelines Act 1962 is amended as follows.

(2) In section 15 (power to place pipe-lines in streets), in subsections (1) to (9)—

(a) for "street" or, in Scotland, "road" substitute "street or, in Scotland, road", and

(b) for "protected street" or, in Scotland, "protected road", wherever occurring, substitute "main road".

(3) For section 15(10) substitute—

"(10) In this section—

"appropriate authority" means—

(a) in England and Wales, the street authority within the meaning of Part III of the New Roads and Street Works Act 1991, and

(b) in Scotland, the road works authority within the meaning of Part IV of that Act;

"carriageway" has the same meaning—

(a) in England and Wales, as in the Highways Act 1980, and

(b) in Scotland, as in the Roads (Scotland) Act 1984;

"main road" means a special road, trunk road or a road classified as a principal road within the meaning of the Highways Act 1980 or the Roads (Scotland) Act 1984;

"road", in Scotland, has the same meaning as in Part IV of the New Roads and Street Works Act 1991; and

"street", in England, has the same meaning as in Part III of that Act.".

(3) For sections 16 and 17 substitute—

"16 Modification of street works or road works provisions

"16 "16 Modification of street works or road works provisions

(1) In relation to undertakers' works in exercise of a power conferred by section 15(1) of this Act, the provisions of Part III or IV of the New Roads and Street Works Act 1991 (street works in England and Wales or road works in Scotland) have effect subject to the provisions of this section.

(2) The provisions of Schedule 4 or 6 of that Act (settlement of plan and section for works in streets or roads with special engineering difficulties) have effect subject as follows—

(a) the period under paragraph 7(2)(b) (period for responding to plan and section as submitted) shall be two months instead of one month;

(b) no modification of a plan and section shall be made which would involve an unacceptable diversion; and

(c) a plan and section shall not be disapproved on the ground that there should be such a diversion.

(3) An arbitrator or arbiter appointed in pursuance of—

(a) paragraph 8(2) of Schedule 4 or 6 of that Act (settlement of plan and section in case of works in street or road with special engineering difficulties), or

(b) section 84(3) or 143(3) of that Act (settlement of necessary measures in case of apparatus affected by certain major works),

shall not provide for an unacceptable diversion.

(4) In subsections (2) and (3) above an "unacceptable diversion" means a lateral diversion of a pipe-line beyond the limits of lateral diversion permissible in relation to it.

(5) No person shall be entitled to payment under section 85 or 144 of the New Roads and Street Works Act 1991 (sharing of costs in case of apparatus affected by certain major works) in respect of measures of his taken in connection with a pipe-line.".

(4) In section 31(1) (power of Minister to remove materials deposited above pipe-line), for "code-regulated works within the meaning of the Public Utilities Street Works Act 1950" substitute "street works within the meaning of Part III of the New Roads and Street Works Act 1991 or, in Scotland, road works within the meaning of Part IV of that Act".

(5) In section 66(1) (general interpretation provisions), for the definition of "emergency works" substitute—

""""emergency works" has the same meaning as in Part III of the New Roads and Street Works Act 1991 or, in Scotland, as in Part IV of that Act;".

New Towns (Scotland) Act 1968 (c. 16)

102 In section 8 of the New Towns (Scotland) Act 1968 (acquisition of land for roads in connection with new towns), in subsection (2) for "a trunk road" substitute "a road for which he is the roads authority".

Sewerage (Scotland) Act 1968 (c. 47)

103 (1) The Sewerage (Scotland) Act 1968 is amended as follows.

(2) In section 41 (breaking open of roads) for the words "Public Utilities Street Works Act 1950" substitute "Part IV of the New Roads and Street Works Act 1991".

(3) In section 59(1) (interpretation) in the definition of "road" for the words "the Public Utilities Street Works Act 1950" substitute "Part IV of the New Roads and Street Works Act 1991".

Town and Country Planning (Scotland) Act 1972 (c. 52)

104 In section 209(2) of the Town and Country Planning (Scotland) Act 1972 (provisions as to telegraphic lines)—

(a) for the words "road, other than a trunk road" substitute "a road for which the Secretary of State is not the roads authority"; and

(b) for the words from "as defined" to the end of that subsection substitute "within the meaning of Part IV of the New Roads and Street Works Act 1991".

Control of Pollution Act 1974 (c. 40)

105 In section 105(1) of the Control of Pollution Act 1974 (interpretation) in the definition of "road" for the words "Public Utilities Street Works Act 1950" substitute "Part IV of the New Roads and Street Works Act 1991".

Local Government (Miscellaneous Provisions) Act 1976 (c. 57)

106 In section 15 of the Local Government (Miscellaneous Provisions) Act 1976 (power of local authorities to survey land), for subsection (4) substitute—

"(4) Where it is proposed to search or bore in pursuance of this section in a street within the meaning of Part III of the New Roads and Street Works Act 1991—

(a) section 55 of that Act (notice of starting date of works), so far as it requires notice to be given to a person having apparatus in the street which is likely to be affected by the works,

(b) section 69 of that Act (requirements to be complied with where works likely to affect another person's apparatus in the street), and

(c) section 82 of that Act (liability for damage or loss caused),

have effect in relation to the searching or boring as if they were street works within the meaning of that Part.".

Development of Rural Wales Act 1976 (c. 75)

107 In Schedule 3 to the Development of Rural Wales Act 1976 (the new towns code)—

(a) in paragraph 1(4)(c) for "a trunk road" substitute "a road for which the Secretary of State is the highway authority", and

(b) in paragraph 2(2) for "a trunk road" substitute "a road for which he is the highway authority".

Water (Scotland) Act 1980 (c. 45)

108 (1) The Water (Scotland) Act 1980 is amended as follows.

(2) In subsection (5) of section 10 (compensation for damage)—

(a) in paragraph (c), for the words from "or managers" to the end of that paragraph substitute "as defined in section 147 of the New Roads and Street Works Act 1991;", and

(b) for paragraph (d) substitute the following—

"(d) road works authority as defined in section 108 of the New Roads and Street Works Act 1991;".

(3) In section 13(5) (bulk supplies of water), for the words "the street works code in the Public Utilities Street Works Act 1950" substitute "the provisions of Part IV of the New Roads and Street Works Act 1991".

(4) In section 23 (power to lay mains), at end insert—

"(4) In the case of works in respect of which notice is required to be given under section 114 of the New Roads and Street Works Act 1991 (notice of starting date of road works), notice duly given to a person in accordance with that section and section 156 of that Act (service of notice) shall be treated as reasonable notice for the purposes of subsection (1) above.".

(5) In section 103 (requirement for all notices to be in writing), after "shall" insert ", subject to section 23(4) of and paragraph 4(1) of Schedule 3 to this Act,"

(6) In section 109(1) (interpretation), in the definition of "road", for the words "Public Utilities Street Works Act 1950" substitute "Part IV of the New Roads and Street Works Act 1991".

(7) In Schedule 3 (provisions as to breaking open streets and laying communication and supply pipes)—

(a) in paragraph 2(2), for the words "section 6 of the Public Utilities Street Works Act 1950" substitute "section 114 of the New Roads and Street Works Act 1991";

(b) in paragraph 4(1) for the words "not less than 72 hours"' substitute the word "such" and at the end of that sub-paragraph add the words "as would require to be given by an undertaker under section 114 of the New Roads and Street Works Act 1991 (notice of starting date of works) in accordance with that section and with section 156 of that Act (service of notice)".

(8) In Schedule 4 (provisions in orders relating to water undertakings)—

(a) in paragraph 5(2), for the words from "or in controlled land" to the end substitute "for the purposes of major road works, major bridge works or major transport works within the meaning of Part IV of the New Roads and Street Works Act 1991"; and

(b) in paragraph 36(b), for the words from "the code" to the end of that paragraph, substitute "Part IV of the New Roads and Street Works Act 1991".

Local Government, Planning and Land Act 1980 (c. 65)

109 In section 167 of the Local Government, Planning and Land Act 1980 (power to survey land), for subsection (7) substitute—

"(7) Where it is proposed to search or bore in pursuance of this section in a street within the meaning of Part III of the New Roads and Street Works Act 1991 or, in Scotland, a road within the meaning of Part IV of that Act—

(a) section 55 or 114 of that Act (notice of starting date of works), so far as it requires notice to be given to a person having apparatus in the street or road which is likely to be affected by the works,

(b) section 69 or 128 of that Act (requirements to be complied with where works likely to affect another person's apparatus in the street or road), and

(c) section 82 or 141 of that Act (liability for damage or loss caused),

have effect in relation to the searching or boring as if they were street works within the meaning of the said Part III or, in Scotland, road works within the meaning of the said Part IV.".

Water Act 1981 (c. 12)

110 In section 6 of the Water Act 1981 (liability of statutory water undertakers for escapes of water), in subsection (7)(c) (meaning of "excepted undertakers"), for sub-paragraphs (iii) and (iv) substitute—

"(iii) any person on whom a right to compensation is conferred by section 82 of the New Roads and Street Works Act 1991;".

British Telecommunications Act 1981 (c. 38)

111 In Schedule 3 to the British Telecommunications Act 1981, in paragraph 74(2) for "177 and 181(7)" substitute "and 177".

New Towns Act 1981 (c. 64)

112 In section 11 of the New Towns Act 1981 (acquisition of land for highways), in subsection (2)(a) (powers of Secretary of State) for "a trunk road" substitute "a road for which he is the highway authority".

Telecommunications Act 1984 (c. 12)

113 (1) In Schedule 2 to the Telecommunications Act 1984 (the telecommunications code), paragraph 1 (interpretation) is amended as follows.

(2) In sub-paragraph (1)—

(a) in the definition of "maintainable highway", in paragraph (a), for the words from the beginning to "1950" substitute "in England and Wales, means a maintainable highway within the meaning of Part III of the New Roads and Street Works Act 1991";

(b) in the definition of "public road", for "the Public Utilities Street Works Act 1950" substitute "Part IV of the New Roads and Street Works Act 1991";

(c) in the definition of "road", for "the meaning given by section 1(3) of the said Act of 1950" substitute "the same meaning as in Part IV of the New Roads and Street Works Act 1991";

(d) in the definition of "street" for "the meaning given by section 1(3) of the said Act of 1950" substitute "the same meaning as in Part III of the New Roads and Street Works Act 1991".

(3) Omit sub-paragraph (4) (which relates to the meaning of the expression "street").

(4) In sub-paragraph (5), for "the Public Utilities Street Works Act 1950" substitute "Part III of the New Roads and Street Works Act 1991".

114 In the same Schedule, in paragraph 2(8)(a) (construction of references to occupier of land)—

(a) for "street" or, in Scotland, "road" in each place where it occurs substitute "street or, in Scotland, road";

(b) in sub-paragraph (ii), for the words from "as references" to the end substitute—

"as references—

in England and Wales or Northern Ireland, to the street managers within the meaning of Part III of the New Roads and Street Works Act 1991 (which for this purpose shall be deemed to extend to Northern Ireland), and

in Scotland, to the road managers within the meaning of Part IV of that Act; and".

115 (1) In the same Schedule, paragraph 9 (street works) is amended as follows.

(2) In sub-paragraph (1), after "over," insert "in, on,", and for "a street" or, in Scotland, "a road" substitute "a street or, in Scotland, a road".

(3) In sub-paragraph (2), for "in a street which is not a maintainable highway" or, in Scotland, "in a road which is not a public road" substitute "in a street which is not a maintainable highway or, in Scotland, a road which is not a public road".

(4) In sub-paragraph (3), for the words from "a special road" to the end substitute "a special road within the meaning of the Roads (Northern Ireland) Order 1980".

Local Government Act 1985 (c. 51)

116 (1) In Schedule 5 to the Local Government Act 1985, paragraph 6 (guidance as to exercise of traffic powers in London and metropolitan counties) is amended as follows.

(2) In sub-paragraph (1) for "other than trunk roads" substitute "other than those for which he is the traffic authority".

(3) In sub-paragraph (3)—

(a) in paragraph (b)(i) for "trunk road" substitute "road for which the Secretary of State is the traffic authority", and

(b) in paragraph (c) for the words "trunk road" substitute the words "road for which he is the traffic authority".

Transport Act 1985 (c. 67)

117 (1) The Transport Act 1985 is amended as follows.

(2) In section 7(12) (application of traffic regulation conditions to local bus services; requirement of consent of Secretary of State) for "a trunk road" substitute "a road for which the Secretary of State is the highway or roads authority".

(3) In section 137(1) (interpretation), omit the definition of "trunk road".

Airports Act 1986 (c. 31)

118 (1) Section 62 of the Airports Act 1986 (provisions as to telecommunications apparatus) is amended as follows.

(2) In subsection (2) (cases in which highway authority or owner of subsoil may require alteration of apparatus), for paragraph (b) substitute—

"(b) for the improvement of the highway where the Secretary of State is not the highway authority,".

(3) In subsection (4) (limit on effect of subsection (2)(b), for "authority's works as defined in Part II of the Public Utilities Street Works Act 1950" substitute "major highway works, major bridge works or major transport works within the meaning of Part III of the New Roads and Street Works Act 1991 or, in Scotland, major works for roads purposes, major bridge works or major transport works within the meaning of Part IV of that Act".

Gas Act 1986 (c. 44)

119 (1) Schedule 4 to the Gas Act 1986 (power of public gas suppliers to break up streets, &c.) is amended as follows.

(2) In paragraphs 1(1), (2) (three times) and 4(1) and (2) for "street or bridge" substitute "street".

(3) In paragraph 2(1) for "highway authority" substitute "street authority".

(4) In paragraph 3(2) for "for the purpose of" substitute "only for the purpose of".

(5) Omit paragraph 5(1).

(6) In paragraph 6, omit the definition of "highway authority" and for the definition of "street" substitute—

""street" and "street authority" have the same meaning as in Part III of the New Roads and Street Works Act 1991.".

(7) In paragraph 7 (adaptations for Scotland)—

(a) for sub-paragraph (b) substitute—

"(b) in paragraph 2(1) for the words "street authority" there shall be substituted the words "road works authority";"

(b) omit sub-paragraph (e); and

(c) for sub-paragraph (f) substitute—

"(f) in paragraph 6, for "street" and "street authority" substitute "road" and "road works authority" and for "Part III" substitute "Part IV".".

120 (1) In Schedule 7 to the Gas Act 1986, paragraph 5 (which relates to the operation of certain provisions of the Pipe-lines Act 1962) is amended as follows.

(2) In sub-paragraph (5), in the definition of "street" for "the Public Utilities Street Works Act 1950" substitute "Part III of the New Roads and Street Works Act 1991".

(3) For sub-paragraph (6) substitute—

"(6) In its application to Scotland this paragraph shall have effect with the substitution for any reference to a street of a reference to a road within the meaning of Part IV of the New Roads and Street Works Act 1991.".

Road Traffic Act 1988 (c. 52)

121 (1) The Road Traffic Act 1988 is amended as follows.

(2) In section 22A(3)(c)(i), omit the words "section 8 of the Public Utilities Street Works Act 1950".

(3) In section 39 (provisions with respect to road safety)—

(a) in subsection (3)(a) (duty of local authority as to study of road accidents), for "trunk roads" substitute "roads for which the Secretary of State is the highway authority (in Scotland, roads authority)";

(b) in subsection (3)(b) (duties as to taking of measures in light of studies), for "roads for which they are the highway authority (in Scotland, local roads authority)" substitute "roads for the maintenance of which they are responsible".

(4) In section 192(1) (general interpretation), for the definition of "highway authority" substitute—

""highway authority", in England and Wales, means—

(a) in relation to a road for which he is the highway authority within the meaning of the Highways Act 1980, the Secretary of State, and

(b) in relation to any other road, the council of the county, metropolitan district or London borough, or the Common Council of the City of London, as the case may be;".

Water Act 1989 (c. 15)

122 (1) The Water Act 1989 is amended as follows.

(2) In section 132(8) (certain works to be treated as emergency works), for "section 39(1) of the Public Utilities Street Works Act 1950" substitute "section 52 of the New Roads and Street Works Act 1991".

(3) In section 189(1) (general interpretation provisions), for the definition of "street" substitute—

""street" has the same meaning as in Part III of the New Roads and Street Works Act 1991;".

(4) In Schedule 19 (provisions as to laying and maintenance of pipes), in paragraphs 3(2) and 10(5)(a) (which relate to emergency works) for "within the meaning of the Public Utilities Street Works Act 1950" substitute "as defined in section 52 of the New Roads and Street Works Act 1991".

Electricity Act 1989 (c. 29)

123 (1) In Schedule 4 to the Electricity Act 1989 (powers of licence-holders), paragraph 1 (street works in England and Wales) is amended as follows.

(2) In sub-paragraph (2) (consent required for placing of certain structures in the street), for the words from "exercisable only" to the end substitute "exercisable only with the consent of the street authority; but such consent shall not be unreasonably withheld".

(3) In sub-paragraph (4) (consent required in certain cases for breaking up or opening street)—

(a) for "a street falling within paragraph (b) or (c) of sub-paragraph (2) above" substitute "a street which is not a maintainable highway", and

(b) for "the person mentioned in that paragraph" substitute "the street authority".

(4) For sub-paragraph (8) (savings) substitute—

"(8) Nothing in sub-paragraph (1) above shall affect the application to any operation of sections 34 to 36 of the Coast Protection Act 1949.".

(5) For sub-paragraph (9) (interpretation) substitute—

"(9) In this paragraph "maintainable highway", "street" and "street authority" have the same meaning as in Part III of the New Roads and Street Works Act 1991.".

124 (1) In the same Schedule, paragraph 2 (road works in Scotland) is amended as follows.

(2) In sub-paragraph (2) (consent required for placing of certain structures in the road), for the words from "exercisable only" to the end substitute "exercisable only with the consent of the road works authority; but such consent shall not be unreasonably withheld".

(3) In sub-paragraph (4) (consent required in certain cases for breaking up or opening road)—

(a) for "a road or bridge falling within paragraph (b) or (c) of sub-paragraph (2) above" substitute "a road which is not a public road", and

(b) for "the person mentioned in that paragraph" substitute "the road works authority".

(4) For sub-paragraph (8) (savings) substitute—

"(8) Nothing in sub-paragraph (1) above shall affect the application to any operation of sections 34 to 36 of the Coast Protection Act 1949.".

(5) For sub-paragraph (9) (interpretation) substitute—

"(9) In this paragraph "public road", "road" and "road works authority" have the same meaning as in Part IV of the New Roads and Street Works Act 1991.".

125 In the same Schedule, in paragraph 12 (interpretation), omit the definitions of "navigation authority" and "railway authority".

Town and Country Planning Act 1990 (c. 8)

126 (1) Section 256 of the Town and Country Planning Act 1990 (provisions as to telecommunications apparatus) is amended as follows.

(2) In subsection (3) (power of local highway authority to require alteration of apparatus) for "highway, other than a trunk road" substitute "highway for which the Secretary of State is not the highway authority".

(3) In subsection (4) (limitation of power under subsection (3)) for "authority's works as defined in Part II of the Public Utilities Street Works Act 1950" substitute "major highway works, major bridge works or major transport works within the meaning of Part III of the New Roads and Street Works Act 1991".

Natural Heritage (Scotland) Act 1991 (c. 28.)

127 In paragraph 5(4) of Schedule 7 to the Natural Heritage (Scotland) Act 1991 (works under drought orders), for "section 39(1) of the Public Utilities Street Works Act 1950" substitute "section 111 of the New Roads and Street Works Act 1991".

SCHEDULE 9

Section 168(2).

REPEALS

Chapter	*Short title*	*Extent of repeal*
1950 c. 39.	Public Utilities Street Works Act 1950.	The whole Act.
1958 c. 30.	Land Powers (Defence) Act 1958.	Section 16(5).
1963 c. 33.	London Government Act 1963.	Section 19.
		In Part III of Schedule 9, in paragraph 1(4), the words "or by or by virtue of the Public Utilities Street Works Act 1950".
1968 c. 73.	Transport Act 1968.	In section 118(12), the words from "or as authorising" to the end.
1972 c. 70.	Local Government Act 1972.	In Schedule 21, paragraph 98.
1973 c. 65.	Local Government (Scotland) Act 1973.	In Schedule 14, paragraph 51.
1978 c. 47.	Civil Liability (Contribution) Act 1978.	In Schedule 1, paragraph 2.
1980 c. 66.	Highways Act 1980.	Section 20.
		In section 21, the words "without prejudice to section 20 above,".
		Section 58(4).
		Section 60.

Chapter	*Short title*	*Extent of repeal*
		Section 64(5).
		Section 90E(4).
		Section 156.
		Section 160.
		Sections 181 to 183.
		In section 184— (a) in subsection (9), the words from "In relation to works" to the end; (b) subsection (14).
		In section 325(1)(d), the word "20,".
		In section 326(2), the word "20,".
		Section 330(3).
		In section 334(1), the words from "but this subsection" to the end.
		Section 340(2)(e).
		In Schedule 23, paragraph 21.
		In Schedule 24, paragraph 5.
1981 c. 38.	British Telecommunications Act 1981.	In Schedule 3, in paragraph 10(5), the words "and 181(9)" and "20(9)".
1982 c. 30.	Local Government (Miscellaneous Provisions) Act 1982.	Section 21(1).
1984 c. 12.	Telecommunications Act 1984.	In section 11(1), the words from the beginning to "; but".
		In Schedule 2— (a) paragraph 1(4); and (b) in paragraph 9(1), the words from "and accordingly" to the end.
		In Schedule 4— (a) in paragraph 3(1)(i), the words "20(9)," and "181(9)"; (b) paragraph 29; (c) paragraph 76(6) and (12); (d) in paragraph 88(1)(b), the words "(except

Chapter	Short title	Extent of repeal
		sections 156, 157 and 159)”.
1984 c. 27.	Road Traffic Regulation Act 1984.	Section 1(2), (4) and (5). In section 3(1), the words from the beginning to “of this Act”. Section 5(2). In section 6— (a) subsection (4); (b) in subsection (6), the words from “and in subsection (4)” to the end. Section 8(2). Section 16(3) and (4). In section 17(6), the words from “and “the date of opening”” to the end. Section 19(3). Section 23(5). In section 34(1), in the opening words, the words “in England and Wales”. Section 55(5). In section 68(1)(a), the reference to section 30. Section 86(4). Section 91. Section 106(8). In section 124(2), the reference to section 30. In section 125(3), the reference to section 30(1). Section 132(6). Section 132A. In Schedule 9— (a) in paragraph 20(1), the reference to section 30; (b) in paragraphs 21 and 23(1)(a), the words

Chapter	*Short title*	*Extent of repeal*
		"other than section 30 of this Act"; (c) in paragraph 27(1), the reference to section 30.
1984 c. 54.	Roads (Scotland) Act 1984.	Section 127.
		Section 133.
		In section 134(1), the words "Without prejudice to section 133 of this Act,".
		In section 143(2)(b)(ii), the words "8 or".
		In Schedule 7, paragraphs 2, 3(a) and (b) and 4.
		In Schedule 9— (a) paragraph 39; (b) paragraph 55(2)(a) and (d) and (3); (c) paragraph 92(4)(c), (e) and (g) to (i); (d) paragraph 93(2) to (22), (23)(a), (24) to (38), (40), (42), (44)(a),(b), (d) and (e) and (45)(b).
		In Schedule 10, paragraph 6.
1985 c. 51.	Local Government Act 1985.	In Schedule 4— (a) paragraph 6, (b) in paragraph 25, the words "156(2)(i)", and (c) paragraph 28.
		In Schedule 5, paragraph 4(2), (3)(a), (6)(b), (8), (9), (11), (12), (15), (19)(a), (29), (33) and (37).
1985 c. 67.	Transport Act 1985.	In section 137(1), the definition of "trunk road".
1986 c. 44.	Gas Act 1986.	In Schedule 4, paragraphs 5(1) and 7(e).
		In Schedule 7, paragraph 2(5).
1988 c. 52.	Road Traffic Act 1988.	In section 22A(3)(c)(i), the words "section 8 of the Public Utilities Street Works Act 1950".

Chapter	*Short title*	*Extent of repeal*
1988 c. 53.	Road Traffic Offenders Act 1988.	In Part I of Schedule 2, the entry relating to section 30(5) of the Road Traffic Regulation Act 1984.
		In Schedule 3— (a) in the entry relating to section 29(3) of the Road Traffic Regulation Act 1984, the words "outside Greater London"; (b) the entry relating to section 30(5) of that Act.
1989 c. 15.	Water Act 1989.	Section 189(5).
		In Schedule 19, paragraph 2(6) and (8).
		In Schedule 25— (a) in paragraph 1(8), the words from "and the Authority" to the end; (b) paragraph 14.
1989 c. 22.	Road Traffic (Driver Licensing and Information Systems) Act 1989.	In section 12(2), the words from "and accordingly" to the end.
		In Schedule 4, paragraph 3(2), (6) and (11).
1989 c. 29.	Electricity Act 1989.	In Schedule 4, in paragraph 12, the definitions of "navigation authority" and "railway authority".
		In Schedule 16— (a) in paragraph 2(6), the words from "and an undertaker" to the end; (b) paragraph 7;(c) paragraph 27.
1990 c. 43	Environmental Protection Act 1990.	In Schedule 8, in paragraph 7, the words from "and in subsection (4)" to the end.

Adapted and published by GRANGIS under the OGL Licence 3.0.

www.nationalarchives.gov.uk/doc/open-government-licence/version/3/

GRANGIS - UK PUBLISHING 2022.

Thank you for taking the time to leave us a review regarding this version

★★★★★

For further inquiries, contact us at:
www.grangis.com / contact@grangis.com

www.ingramcontent.com/pod-product-compliance
Lightning Source LLC
LaVergne TN
LVHW060212210926
848481LV00008B/2709
* 9 7 9 8 8 8 5 5 9 0 2 9 7 *